James Madison

and the Creation of the American Republic

James Madison
1751–1836

James Madison

and the Creation of the American Republic

Jack N. Rakove

Edited by Oscar Handlin

 HarperCollins*Publishers*

Acknowledgment

Frontispiece photo: used with the permission of the Library of Congress

Library of Congress Cataloging-in-Publication Data

Rakove, Jack N.
    James Madison and the creation of the American Republic /
    Jack N. Rakove.
        p.   cm.—(The Library of American biography)
    ISBN 0-673-39994-X
    1. Madison, James, 1751–1836. 2. Presidents—United States—
Biography. 3. United States—Politics and government—1783–1809.
4. United States—Politics and government—1809–1817. I. Title.
II. Series.
E342.R35   1990   973.5′1′092—dc20   89-24350
[B]   CIP

9 — EBL — 98

for Alex and Alice Scharf

Editor's Preface

James Madison left college just as the American Revolution began to stir; he completed his second term as president when the divisive War of 1812 confirmed the nation's independence. Thus, Madison participated in the most critical political developments of the first half-century of the United States.

As a young Princeton graduate, Madison carried into Virginia politics well-formed ideas about the nature of the state and its relation to society, gleaned from wide reading and stimulating courses. The actual experience of forming a government and then getting it to work, however, revealed the shortcomings of book learning. He and other Americans faced immense tasks—uniting a nation that extended over immense distances; and forming a free government that would rule by the consent of the governed. No precedent, ancient or modern, provided a guide.

The personal and national challenge to accomplish these tasks came during Madison's participation in the Constitutional Convention of 1787. There he took the initial steps to translate into reality the general ideas about politics derived from his studies. Madison recognized, at that point, that reality required compromise to bring people of different backgrounds together. He also recognized that the Constitution, as ratified, remained an abstract framework. To make it work required further effort and a process of adaptation that significantly changed the way in which the government functioned. Madison participated actively in those efforts as a member of Congress, as a party leader, and finally as president. In all those roles, he learned to appreciate the distance between theory and reality. Professor Rakove's thoughtful book traces those steps in vivid detail.

Oscar Handlin

Author's Preface

In 1831, not long after his eightieth birthday, James Madison received a letter from a popular New York writer who wanted to know whether the retired statesman would be willing to preapre a sketch of his autobiography. The brief memoir Madison drafted contained no ringing statement of principles that he hoped history would vindicate, no proud recollections of victories won, no poignant reflections on the occasional defeats in a political career of forty years. Madison's sketch provided only a bare outline of his public life. That was the way he wanted it. The biography of a public man, he felt, should be a record of what he had done, not a gossipy tale of ambition and desire, disappointment and education. In his own lifetime he took care to preserve his political papers as well as to insure that the details of his private life would remain hidden from prosperity. After his death in 1836, his widow, Dolley Madison, honored his wishes and protected his privacy. It is the public man alone whom we can know with any confidence.

Even had Madison been more gracious toward the curiosity of later generations, however, our impressions of him might not be very different. For, in truth, it was only in the conduct of public affairs that his deepest traits and interests found expression. Force of personality alone could never have elevated him to the distinguished rank he holds among the founders of the American republic. Of the three men who preceded him as president, Madison lacked the stern but charismatic dignity of Washington, the obstreperous and restless temper of John Adams, and the warmth and charm of his good friend, Thomas Jefferson. Nor did his personality cause him to shine among his contemporaries. He was less bold than Alexander Hamilton, less cosmopolitan than Benjamin Franklin, less ambitious than Robert Morris or James Wilson. Thomas

Paine was a far more effective writer, and Patrick Henry and Richard Henry Lee, his Virginia rivals, far more stirring orators.

Such was the power of his intellect and the creativity of his political thought, however, that Madison has rightly come "to be regarded," the historian Michael Kammen observed, "as the most profound, original, and far-seeing among all his peers." In the task of creating the national republic, he had many partners, but few equals. From his arrival at the Continental Congress in 1780 until his retirement from the presidency in 1817, Madison played a key role in every significant political development: the earliest efforts to amend the Articles of Confederation, the adoption of the Federal Constitution of 1787, the framing of the Bill of Rights, the organization of the first opposition party, and the long diplomatic and military struggle that ended with the War of 1812, America's second war of independence.

In the upsurge of Madisonian scholarship of recent decades, it is still Madison the thinker, rather than Madison the politican or leader, who has commanded attention and applause. His greatest contributions to the new republic, it is often suggested, were more those of the engaged intellectual than those of the creative statesman. Yet, in his own way, he was an extremely adept and skillful leader. If Madison's style of leadership was destined to give way before the mass politics of the nineteenth century, it still served him quite well in the world that the Founding Fathers inhabited. Understanding how Madison and many of his contemporaries combined a deeply principled and intellectual attitude toward politics with the responsibility of conducting the affairs of state is essential to understanding both their remarkable achievements and the limitations of their vision.

Jack N. Rakove

Contents

James Madison

and the Creation of the American Republic

CHAPTER ONE

Piedmont and Princeton

James Madison was born on March 16, 1751, into the class of landed Virginia planters who expected to govern their colony as a matter of right. His paternal great-great-grandfather, John Maddison, had settled in the colony in the mid-seventeenth century, an early arrival among a wave of immigrants whose families ruled Virginia for the next two centuries. A ship's carpenter of some ambition, John Maddison had managed to pay the costs of transporting a dozen indentured servants to England's first successful colony in North America. By 1653 he was entitled, under Virginia's headright system, to six hundred acres of land, fifty for each immigrant whose passage he had paid. By the time of his death, around 1683, he held another thirteen hundred acres. In the early Chesapeake, where life was (as Thomas Hobbes put it) "nasty, brutish, and short," the first Maddison was one of the lucky winners who laid a foundation for his descendants' prosperity.

His son and grandsons added substantially to the family holdings. Ambrose Madison—John Maddison's grandson—carried his branch of the family into the Virginia piedmont, settling in Orange County after his marriage to Frances Taylor in 1721. Their only son, James, the President's father, was born there in 1723.

Ambrose died in 1732. Though as sole male heir James might have married early, not until September 1749 did he take as his bride Nelly Conway, seventeen years old and the youngest

1

daughter of a merchant-planter of Caroline County. Their first son and eldest child, James Madison, Jr., was born a year and a half later at the plantation of his maternal grandmother. Ten other children followed until the last was born in 1774, when Nelly was forty-two. Seven of her children lived to adulthood, while Nelly herself survived the rigors of childbirth to reach the ripe age of ninety-seven. The longevity of the Madisons suggests something about the improving living conditions of the provincial society into which James Madison, the favored son of a prominent family, was born.

His parents had both lost their fathers at an early age, and perhaps memories of their grief made them indulgent. James Madison, Sr., was also the wealthiest landowner in Orange County, and his eldest son could rest assured that his own prospects were quite secure. Madison's relations with his parents were both respectful and affectionate. Even when, in his early twenties, he experienced a period of uncertainty about his own purposes in life, there is no record of parental pressure on him. Later, when the Revolution called James to his political vocation, his father provided all the financial support James needed, at a time when the salary of a public official fell far below the required expenses.

By his early teens, Madison was acquiring the intellectual earnestness that marked him ever after. Living on an isolated plantation (with younger siblings to look after rather than older ones to pester), he welcomed the opportunity, at age eleven, to attend the school kept by Donald Robertson in neighboring King and Queen County. Schooling of any kind was scarce in Virginia, but Robertson, a University of Edinburgh graduate, kept a school as rigorous as its new pupil was serious. Among other subjects, Madison studied logic, philosophy, mathematics, astronomy, and French (with a Scots burr). He spent five years there, and another two being tutored at the family plantation, Montpelier, by the Reverend Thomas Martin. In 1769, at Martin's recommendation, the Madisons agreed that James would continue his studies at the College of New Jersey (later Princeton University) rather than Virginia's own William and Mary.

Madison, a sickly youth, feared the unhealthy environment of Williamsburg, but his decision to attend the College of New Jersey certainly reflected an awareness that it was a far better institution. A year before Madison matriculated, a prominent Scottish clergyman, John Witherspoon, had been named its new president. Witherspoon had earned a reputation defending orthodox Calvinism against more moderate elements of the Scottish Presbytery, and he was called to Princeton in part to pursue his campaign within the College. In America, however, he exerted his greatest influence over his scholars (as undergraduates were once called) in philosophy, not religion. Witherspoon remade the college into a major outpost of the Scottish enlightenment, introducing his students to the moral philosophy of Frances Hutcheson, Thomas Reid, and Lord Kames, and the social science of Adam Ferguson, Adam Smith, and David Hume.

Many students leave college with only vague memories of what they have read; over time their notion of what their education meant is reduced to nostalgia for a circle of friends, recollections of a particular teacher whose interests somehow sparked their own, and odd memories of books and authors. Madison retained much more. He was an intense and ambitious student who graduated a year early and then stayed on to pursue further studies. Yet it would be fruitless to examine his education too closely for clues to his later thought. The political views he absorbed in college were commonplace throughout America; it took the experience of revolution to give his academic ideas the focus they needed. The years at Princeton were important in a more general way. They reinforced Madison's intellectual bent and gave him knowledge that he could draw upon as later occasions arose. He never lost the love of books he acquired there, nor his faith, typical of the Enlightenment, in the capacity of reason to deal with human affairs.

Yet a liberal education had one drawback. It left him ill-prepared for the life he faced upon his return to Montpelier. Only in retirement would he grow content to act the part of gentleman farmer. But the routines of planter society held little appeal for a young man of twenty-one, more interested in books than in crops. Horse racing, too, was something he learned to enjoy only later in life. It is difficult to imagine the earnest graduate of 1771 relishing a good match race and the betting that accompanied it in the same way that many of the younger gentry of Virginia did. His father was still actively managing the family's lands, and since Madison was as yet uninterested in marriage, he had no reason to establish a plantation of his own. In truth, he was at loose ends. On the eve of the Revolution, he was a young man possessed of wealth, education, excellent prospects, and no plans. When his college friend William Bradford wrote to complain that "I leave Nassau Hall [at Princeton] with the same regret that a fond son would feel who parts with an indulgent mother to tempt the dangers of the sea," Madison knew what he meant.

Poor health kept Madison from worrying too much about a vocation. Writing to Bradford in November 1772, he confessed that his "sensations for many months past have intimated to me not to expect a long or healthy life." Though he hoped to recover his health, he felt little inclination "to set about any thing that is difficult in acquiring and useless in possessing after one has exchanged Time for Eternity." His life was probably in far less danger than he believed. But his anxieties were real enough, and they contributed to his striking lack of ambition.

His isolation "in an obscure corner" of the land was also irksome. Madison envied his friend Bradford, whose residence in Philadelphia placed him "at the Fountain-Head of Political and Literary Intelligence." While Bradford could return to Princeton for postgraduate study, Madison had to content himself with writing President Witherspoon for guidance about additional reading. And when Bradford mentioned a literary controversy that Witherspoon had sparked, Madison had to confess that a single notice in a Philadelphia newspaper was all he knew of it. "These things seldom reach Virginia," he reported, "and when they do I am out of the way of them."

Bradford was not only better situated than Madison, he was also choosing a profession. In August 1773 Bradford reported that the choices included religion, law, medicine, or commerce.

His own preferences, he noted, were strongly for law, whose only drawback (as always) was that "it is overstocked"; but he was anxious for his friend's opinion.

Madison struck a suitably sober note in response. He advised Bradford to consult his own genius rather than the "comparative Excellence" of the other pursuits. On the whole, he concluded, law seemed the most attractive field: "It is a sort of general Lover that woos all the Muses and Graces." Was its appeal also wooing Madison? After learning that Bradford, having followed his advice, found "but little of that disagreeable dryness I was taught to expect" in reading law, Madison reported that he, too, had "procured" some law books. But his own intentions were modest: "I intend myself to read Law occasionally." For Madison, such knowledge implied no choice of a vocation; it was only a necessary part of an education, leading as it did to an understanding of "the principles & Modes of Government."

Madison's own interest in politics, however, seemed slight. He understood the basic constitutional issues that had been driving Britain and its American colonies apart since the Stamp Act of 1765. And there was no question where his allegiances lay. Most of the students at Princeton believed the colonies should resist Parliament's attempts to tax His Majesty's loyal American subjects; President Witherspoon was himself a vigorous Whig who later signed the Declaration of Independence. Yet Madison's few surviving letters from the early 1770s ignored politics entirely. Even as late as January 1774, after Bradford had sent him a newspaper account of the Boston Tea Party, Madison replied in measured tones, "I wish Boston may conduct matters with as much discretion as they seem to do with boldness." A few further reflections exhausted his interest. "But away with Politicks!" he abruptly declared, reverting to a more familiar role. "Let me address you as a Student and Philosopher & not as a Patriot now." Revolution lay just around the corner, but Madison still preferred the pedantic themes of the schoolboy.

One political subject did arouse his passions in a way that linked the ideals of the scholar with the future concerns of the politician: religious toleration. Like most of the colonies, Virginia had an established church—the Church of England. By European standards, its powers did not amount to much, nor did the Church command the intense loyalty of the population. Anglicanism, by its very nature, did not demand rigorous obervance from its communicants; and Virginians, by their very nature, did not offer it. Equally important was the fact that Virginia was not religiously homogeneous. Large numbers of Presbyterians were settling in the backcountry, many of them Scots-Irish immigrants whose distaste for the Church of England ran as deep as their thirst for the whiskey they contributed to American life. Then, too, enthusiasm and strict Calvinism set a growing number of Baptists well apart from the polite forms and rational beliefs of the Anglicans.

The arrest in a neighboring county of several dissenting Baptists for preaching without a license drew from Madison the strongest political statements he would make before the Revolution. Writing to Bradford, Madison denounced the Anglican "Imps" he blamed for this persecution and then confessed that he no longer had the "patience to hear talk or think of any thing relative to this matter, for I have squabbled and scolded abused and ridiculed so long about it . . . that I am without common patience." Once again, Madison found reason to envy his friend in Pennsylvania, where religious toleration had taken root with the very founding of the Quaker colony a century earlier. How different remained the situation in Virginia. When Madison next wrote his friend in early April 1774, he predicted that the coming session of the Virginia assembly would fail to take appropriate measures in support of private rights of conscience.

In fact, the legislators who met at Williamsburg in May 1774 faced a more serious threat to the liberties of Virginians. They had hardly assembled when they learned that Parliament had approved an act closing the port of Boston until restitution was made for the tea that had been brewed in their harbor the previous December. When the legislators resolved to call a colony-wide day of prayer and fasting on June 1, the day the Boston Port Act would take effect, the royal governor ordered the assembly dissolved. A rump session of the House of Burgesses met in Raleigh's Tavern a day later and took the first measures that committed the most populous and wealthy of Britain's American provinces to support its "sister colony" of Massachusetts.

Madison learned of the crisis even before the burgesses. In April he had left Montpelier to take his brother William north to school, a trip that enabled him to visit Philadelphia. There he witnessed the frantic political activity that followed the first word of the Boston Port Act. By the time Madison returned to Montpelier in late June, the entire continent was in ferment.

For Madison, as for other young men that fateful summer, the rush of public events was about to overtake both the commitments and uncertainties of private life. Had the Revolution not intervened, a mature Madison would probably still have taken a seat in the House of Burgesses and risen to the same position of responsibility that Thomas Jefferson, eight years his senior, already enjoyed. Plantation life could never have satisfied Madison, and his family's status could have given him ready access to office. Yet there was a world of difference between entering a legislature charged with overseeing the parochial concerns of a provincial society or finding oneself thrust into politics in the midst of a revolution. For Madison—as for John Adams, James Wilson, John Jay, and many others—the coming of the Revolution provided opportunities to discover talents they otherwise would never have known existed.

CHAPTER TWO

Politics as a Vocation

❖
❖

The political storm that broke over America in 1774 had been a decade in the making. The American Revolution had many causes, and the mix of concerns that led the colonists to renounce their allegiance to Great Britain varied from place to place and even from one individual to another. Yet at the core of the dispute lay one simple issue: What authority, if any, could the British Parliament justly exercise over America?

This question had first been posed in terms of the right of Parliament to impose taxes on America. In the Revenue Act of 1764, the Stamp Act of 1765, and the Townshend duties of 1767, the British government sought ways to make the colonists shoulder part of the financial burden of maintaining the enormous empire it had acquired with its victory over France in the Seven Years' War (1756–1763). Americans resented these requests because they felt they had already borne their fair share of the war's costs; but more to the point, they argued, such taxes could be imposed only by the free acts of their own assemblies, not by a Parliament in which they were not—nor ever could be—represented.

A debate that began over taxation quickly escalated into a dispute over representation and soon reached even higher levels of constitutional principle. Thoughtful colonists began to question whether they should obey any laws that Parliament enacted—even the Navigation Acts, which had regulated American commerce since the time of John Maddison. By the early 1770s, radical American spokesmen argued that they owed allegiance not to Parliament but only to the Crown, and even then only if King George III treated his colonial subjects as favorably as he did the residents of Britain.

What was ultimately at dispute in this controversy was the same issue that would preoccupy James Madison in the 1780s. How could a great and expanding empire so divide the powers of government as to secure both the general interests of the whole and the particular rights of its many parts? British leaders asserted that sovereignty—the ultimate right to rule—could not be divided. Together, Parliament and Crown were the supreme governing power, whose decisions the colonists had to obey. Against this view, the Americans struggled to develop a theory of federalism, to distinguish what Parliament could and could not do. When the British insisted that this was an impossibility, Americans were forced to deny that Parliament could rightly claim any authority at all.

Only in 1774 did imperial officials learn just how many colonists supported this conclusion. In response to the Boston Tea Party, the British government decided to make an example of Massachusetts (which has never been an easy place to govern) by closing the port of Boston and radically altering the colony's government. The Coercive Acts of 1774 sought to force the descendants of the Puritans to repent their political sins, while teaching colonists elsewhere the costs of defiance. Instead, masses of Americans began first to assert the rights of resistance and then to calculate the benefits of independence.

When the crisis broke in 1774, James Madison was still one among thousands of Americans whose support of resistance had yet to be converted into actual participation in "the common cause." Back at Montpelier in late June, he again found himself in "possession of my customary enjoyments Solitude and Contemplation." Yet for the first time, his letters to Bradford betrayed a serious interest in politics. Madison wrote as a firm, even militant, Whig. He criticized those who favored avoiding all preparations for war until the British government could consider the petitions it would receive from the Continental Congress that was to gather in Philadelphia in September. "Delay on our part emboldens our adversaries and improves their schemes," he noted, "while it abates the ardor of Americans . . . and affords opportunity to our secret enemies to disseminate discord & disunion." Later, when Congress adjourned without recommending military preparations, Madison proudly reported that companies of citizen soldiers were forming in many Virginia counties and "voluntarily subjecting themselves to military discipline that they may be expert & prepared against a time of Need."

Yet Madison's involvement in revolutionary activities lagged behind his opinions. In December 1774 he was elected a member of the Orange County Committee of Safety, one of hundreds of such bodies formed to carry out the commercial boycott adopted by Congress in October. Since his father was chairman of the Committee, however, Madison's appointment marked no sudden unleashing of political ambition. In October 1775, half a year after war had begun in Massachusetts, Madison was commissioned as colonel of the county militia, though again, his father already commanded the county's troops. In fact, Madison's frail health made it unlikely that he would play an active military role.

In the spring of 1776, however, he was elected a delegate to the Virginia Provincial Convention, the colony's effective legislature since the royal government had collapsed the previous summer. No doubt his family's prestige aided his election. At age twenty-five, James Madison was about to find a vocation.

Still politically inexperienced, Madison left Montpelier knowing he would participate in momentous events. Talk of independence was widespread. Thomas Paine's inflammatory pamphlet *Common Sense* had been published in January, and its blunt arguments for separation had deflated the faint hopes of reconciliation many colonists still harbored.

Nor had recent events encouraged anyone to hope that the dispute could end amicably. Neither Congress nor the government of Lord North seemed willing to retreat from entrenched positions. Meanwhile, each battle fought on American soil reinforced the militant patriotism that first swept the country in

April 1775, when anxious riders carried news of the skirmishes at Lexington and Concord from towns to hamlets to outlying farms and plantations. By early 1776, independence was becoming a question of timing more than policy.

For the members who rode to Williamsburg in heavy rains that ended an unusually cold, early spring, that time had arrived. The three provinces to the south had already voted for independence; similar action by Virginia would have a powerful impact in the middle colonies, where public opinion still seemed divided. On May 15, with little debate or soul-searching, the Convention instructed its delegates in Congress to propose a declaration of independence, the negotiation of foreign alliances, and the completion of articles of confederation to bind the colonies in a formal union. In Philadelphia that same day, Congress called upon the colonies to replace the extralegal network of committees and conventions that had ruled America since 1774 with duly constituted, legal governments whose powers were to be "exerted under the authority of the people." This act gave Americans the opportunity to decide exactly what forms of government they wished to live under. An exuberant John Adams captured the mood of many of his countrymen when he noted that they "had been sent into life at a time when the greatest lawgivers of antiquity would have wished to have lived."

Madison understood what Adams meant. But as a political newcomer, he was in no position to play a major role in constitution making in Virginia. The revolution produced no dramatic turnover in the state's ruling elite. When, in late May, the Provincial Convention began drafting a new constitution, a select group of men whose prestige was sometimes resented but rarely challenged firmly guided its work. Watching them manage the wide range of tasks the Convention confronted, Madison gained his first lessons in legislative politics. And his potential talents were in turn assessed by men who knew that the war would require the recruitment of a new generation of leaders.

Among the Convention's leaders, none would support Madison's career more than its president, Edmund Pendleton.

As the youngest son of a planter of middling status, Pendleton had lacked the birthright in land and slaves that set the colony's ruling elite apart; he turned instead to law and politics to further his career. He had sat continuously in the House of Burgesses since 1752, earning a reputation for amiability, candor, and attention to detail. No one was better at framing the compromises and coalitions that legislative influence required.

Two other delegates caught Madison's eye. George Mason enjoyed all the advantages of birth that Pendleton lacked and was equally a force to reckon with. His was by far the more powerful intellect. From his pen had come some of the most cogent statements of the American case. Casting himself in the role of the virtuous republican, a man of absolute moral independence, his influence rested on sheer force of reputation and intellect. His opinions carried the greater weight because everyone knew how much Mason preferred the privacy of his plantation at Gunston Hall to the tedium of public life.

And then there was Patrick Henry. No one would ever accuse this legendary orator of having the tactical skills of Pendleton or the virtue and intellect of Mason. To his detractors, Henry seemed just the sort of demagogue a revolution could be expected to produce. As Madison would learn, Henry's powers of persuasion made him a formidable opponent.

These three men were the great figures in the Convention, but the rich pool of talent that enabled Virginia to dominate American politics over the next half century ran far deeper. The most distinguished of these leaders was George Washington, already serving as commander-in-chief of the Continental army. But the Virginia delegation at Congress also included some of the colony's other great men: George Wythe, a brilliant jurist; Richard Henry Lee, a patriot as militant as Henry; Carter Braxton and Benjamin Harrison, spokesmen for the colony's more conservative planters; and Thomas Jefferson, the great proponent of enlightened reform. Whatever their rivalries and differences, these men shared the values of a political culture sanctioned by time and custom. They, their families, and their class had governed Virginia for a century; no group of leaders faced the ferment of revolution more confidently.

Had they been less certain of their authority, they might never have accepted the liberal provisions written into their new constitution by Mason, its principal draftsman. The constitution adopted on June 29, 1776, though still too conservative for Jefferson, illustrated what American republican principles meant in practice. Members of both houses of the assembly would serve only a year, with the expectation that frequent elections would keep them dependent on the will of the people. The executive branch was purposely kept weak: the governor, annually elected by the legislature, was to be only an agent of its will.

Madison as yet had nothing to contribute to most of the issues the Convention considered. But he was better prepared when the members debated the accompanying Declaration of Rights that stated the general values upon which the constitution rested. The first of many such bills of rights that Americans produced, it voiced the ideals that gave the Revolutionary era its distinctive tone. Like the constitution, it was largely the work of Mason; but in the wording of its final provision, James Madison made his first contribution to American republicanism.

The issue that moved Madison was religious liberty. Mason's text declared that "all men shou'd enjoy the fullest Toleration in the Exercise of Religion, according to the Dictates of Conscience." That seemed liberal enough until one asked whether "toleration" implied only that free religious belief was a *privilege* that the state could grant or revoke, not an inherent *right* that all possessed. Madison himself already believed in the strict separation of church and state. But when the delegates refused to disestablish the Anglican church, he moved to replace the offer of toleration with the unequivocal recognition that "all men are equally entitled to the free exercise of religion." With Pendleton's support—itself a sign of the amendment's reasonable character—Madison's change won approval; and its adoption laid the intellectual basis for disestablishment. This was Madison's one significant achievement at the Convention.

The Convention adjourned on July 5, unaware that Congress had approved the Declaration of Independence the day before. Madison spent the summer at Montpelier, but in mid-October, when the Convention reassembled as the new House of Delegates, he returned to Williamsburg. Still learning the ropes, he played no more conspicuous a role than before. But at this session Madison came into direct contact with Thomas Jefferson, already a recognized leader in Virginia's revolutionary elite. The elder son of a wealthy Albemarle County planter who had died when he was only fourteen, Jefferson had studied law at William and Mary under George Wythe. Like Madison, he loved his books and valued the solitude of his own thoughts. Jefferson's intellect was the wider ranging, and by temperament he was the more optimistic of the two. Over time, Madison would become the more original thinker, and perhaps the more realistic.

Their common ideas about religious liberty formed the original basis of their friendship. As members of the Committee on Religion, they were entrusted with the petitions calling for disestablishment received from dissenters throughout the state. The strong resolutions that Jefferson wrote and the committee endorsed, however, were too advanced for most of the legislators. Instead they adopted a compromise, which merely exempted members of dissenting sects from having to pay taxes to support the established church.

From this episode Madison learned a valuable lesson about legislative politics. It was one thing to secure agreement on a broad statement of principle, as he had earlier done with his amendment to the Declaration of Rights. But translating a general commitment into actual legislation was another matter entirely. On the assembly floor, Pendleton had not challenged the liberal principles on which the committee's recommendations rested. But by whittling away at the specific proposals they had reported, he succeeded in protecting the Church's privileged position.

Madison's other activities at this session involved the routine committee work that drove many to distraction. But unlike others whose first taste of politics sent them galloping to their plantations, he was already finding in public life the sense of purpose he had previously missed. When new elections for the House of Delegates were held in April 1777, he announced his candidacy.

Elections in eighteenth-century Virginia involved more than simply tallying the voters' preferences. For people who lived on dispersed plantations, they were great social events. Before the voters openly declared their choice at the table where the county clerks kept the pollbook, the candidates treated them to drinks and other refreshments. "Swilling the planters with bumbo," as it was called, was not an art at which the prim Madison excelled. Besides, how did this promote the "moderation, temperance, frugality, and virtue" that the Declaration of Rights had asked of Virginians? Regarding the "personal solicitation" of voters and "the corrupting influence of spirituous liquors" as "equally inconsistent with the purity of moral and of republican principles," Madison refrained from the customary practice. His opponent, who kept a tavern as well as a plantation, felt no such scruples, and carried the poll. An appeal to the assembly's committee on elections was unavailing. As a result, Madison spent the year 1777 at home, no doubt catching up on his reading.

Yet he had not been forgotten by his former colleagues at Williamsburg. In November 1777 the assembly elected him to fill a vacancy on the eight-member Council of State which served as an advisory board to the governor. In theory, the council shared the subordinate status of the executive branch. In practice, it had to consider many and weighty problems. For by January 1778, when Madison returned to Williamsburg, the experience of war was uncovering major discrepancies between republican ideals and the actual burdens of governing. The high idealism of 1776 had been muted. In the place of heady debates about constitutions and rights, the public agenda was now dominated by the mundane but urgent concerns of maintaining a war entering its fourth year with no sign of ending.

Americans did have some cause for optimism that winter. The campaign of 1777 had ended gloriously when a British army led by General John Burgoyne had surrendered at Saratoga,

New York, after slogging its way across the Adirondacks. This victory not only removed the danger of invasion from Canada, it also brought France into the war as an ally of the new republic. But these events had ominous consequences for the South. The British henceforth concentrated their operations between Georgia and Virginia, straining the resources of the still inexperienced governments that had to mobilize against the onslaught.

Upon his return to Williamsburg, Madison took lodgings with the Reverend James Madison, his second cousin and the new president of William and Mary. At his first appearance at the Council on January 14, he found in attendance four of his colleagues and Governor Patrick Henry. It was a typical day of business. After Madison was duly sworn to office, the council issued a routine warrant for the purchase of provisions. It next read a letter from Congress which reported that General Washington's army, then in its bitter encampment at Valley Forge, "must either *Starve Disolve or Disperse*" unless immediately provided with adequate supplies of food. The council ordered the Continental commissary to purchase "all the pork Beef & Bacon that can be procured" and arrange for its prompt shipment to the army.

The Council then took up a more adventurous item, approving a plan to send a party of thirty men to New Orleans. There they were to obtain supplies needed at Fort Pitt (modern Pittsburgh), to learn what they could about English activities along the Mississippi, and to discuss various matters with the Spanish territorial governor, Bernardo de Gálvez. For Virginia the control of the interior of the American continent was a major concern. By the vague terms of its royal charter, the state claimed title to much of the territory across the Appalachians. Other states wanted these claims transferred to the Union through the creation of a national domain whose sale would pay much of the cost of the war. As a native of the Virginia frontier, Madison already appreciated the state's interest in the control of this staggering treasure of land.

Most of the time he faithfully devoted to the council over the next two years, however, was spent addressing these questions of supplies that opened his first day's session. Meeting six days a week, the council had acquired duties far greater than those envisioned by the constitution makers of 1776, simply because it sat year round while the legislature met for only limited periods. Out of necessity, the assembly delegated an increasing range of tasks to the council. The most urgent involved raising men and supplies, collecting such taxes as the assembly dared to levy, and carrying out the miscellaneous chores that the conduct of war required. These problems preoccupied Madison in 1778 and 1779.

His term coincided with the collapse of the financial and logistical policies that Congress and the states had pursued since 1775. Rather than pay the costs of war through heavy, immediate taxation, both levels of government printed bills of exchange—paper money—to defray current costs. In theory the value of these bills, in comparison to specie (hard money), would be maintained by making them payable for taxes. By late 1777, the scale and duration of the war were crushing these expectations. Shortages of all kinds of goods drove prices up, while the expenses of war kept the printing presses rolling at a pace that no scheme of taxation could match. By 1779 two hundred dollars in paper currency were worth one in specie, and no check to the inflationary spiral was in sight.

The collapse of the currency also made it more difficult to keep the Continental army clothed and fed. Farmers and artisans refused to exchange the products of their farms and shops for the worthless paper that military commissaries thrust into their hands. The virtue of the republican citizen—his willingness to subordinate private interest to public good—was being sorely tested by unrelenting inflation. By the summer of 1779, a crisis of supply as well as finance threatened the new republic's ability to maintain a fighting army in the field.

The two years that Madison spent on the Council of State were thus an education in the realities of government. Membership was not quite a year-round obligation: from midsummer to early fall he was back at Montpelier, avoiding the "sickly season" when malaria-bearing mosquitoes came swarming from ponds and swamps throughout the tidewater. But when Madison was at Williamsburg, his attendance was faithful. Wrestling daily with the problems of maintaining the war effort, he came to suspect that virtue alone could not sustain the Revolution. As a member of an executive body charged with implementing the assembly's vague will, he began to recognize the limits of legislative supremacy. And as the youngest councillor, he was in a fine position to impress more influential men—such as Pendleton and Jefferson, who succeeded Henry as governor in 1779—with his abilities.

They liked what they saw. In 1779 the Virginia delegation to Congress was in disarray. Its most capable members had retired, and those who remained at Philadelphia were lackluster. Among the four new members whom the assembly elected on December 14, 1779, was James Madison. Many others who had this honor unexpectedly thrust upon them found ways to avoid attending or to return home as soon as they could. Not Madison—he accepted the appointment immediately and began making plans to return to Philadelphia. At age twenty-eight, he was launching a career in national politics that would end only when he retired from the presidency thirty-seven years later.

CHAPTER THREE

Congressman

Many delegates accepted election to Congress reluctantly, aware that service in America's first national government meant absence from all the private concerns disrupted by the war. James Madison, however, had few of the personal cares that beset his new colleagues. He left behind no family whose welfare would nag at his conscience, no plantation or office whose management would suffer from his absence. His father's wealth gave him financial security, and Philadelphia was a city Madison knew well. Only an unusually cold winter kept him in Virginia until early March 1780. He would not return home until December 1783, having spent almost four uninterrupted years dealing with the problems of national government.

Congress no longer enjoyed the confidence it had commanded in 1774 and 1775, when it was hailed as "the collected wisdom" of America. When Madison presented his credentials on March 20, Congress was in the midst of overhauling its entire policy for sustaining the war. Just two days earlier, it had adopted a plan to devalue its massive $200 million debt to $5 million. Many delegates feared this scheme would never work, and they also worried about other recent decisions shifting the burden of provisioning the Continental army to the states. The experiment seemed doubly risky at a time when the British seemed poised to regain control of the southernmost parts of the Union.

Other factors contributed to the erosion of congressional authority. A bitter dispute over foreign policy had preoccupied Congress during 1779, ultimately spilling over into newspaper polemics that sullied its reputation further. Reputation might have mattered less had the authority of Congress rested on a secure foundation. But the Articles of Confederation that had been drafted in 1777 remained unratified. Maryland refused to ratify until those states claiming title to western lands ceded their rights, thereby permitting the creation of a national domain whose sale would offer a painless method of paying the costs of independence.

Madison did not underestimate these problems. His two years on the Council of State had taught him that the authority of the states was almost as fragile as that of Congress. Yet his early impressions of Congress were hardly generous. His first report to Governor Jefferson portrayed a body that "from a defect of adequate statesmen" was "more likely to fall into wrong measures and of less weight to enforce right ones."

Madison immediately undertook the prosaic duties of a delegate. His juniority entitled him to a place on the Admiralty Board, and election to other committees soon followed. Although Congress met daily for debate and decision, the delegates spent much of their time in the various committees that discharged Congress's routine chores. There was no glamor here, but diligence and sound judgment even on minor problems could win respect. Familiarity with the daily business could also bring influence, especially in a small body—rarely more than three dozen men—whose membership changed constantly.

All members of Congress were subject to the tug of competing loyalties. As a *delegate* from Virginia, Madison was obliged to protect its immediate interests. When members from other states argued that Virginia should yield its territorial claims, he had to defend the terms upon which the assembly insisted its cession would be made. Yet on other occasions, Madison had to address his constituents as a *member* of Congress. If they complained that the northern states had failed to relieve the South from the British offensive, he had to explain why they should still support the Union that Congress embodied. Within Congress, too, he learned that one could lose influence by being too faithful to constituents' interests.

The western lands issue was Madison's greatest concern during his first year in Congress, and this in turn plunged him into maneuvers to bring the Articles of Confederation to final completion. Madison roomed in the boarding house kept by a widow with the unlikely name of Mary House. This brought him into close contact with several New York delegates, who believed that the recovery of congressional power had to begin with ratification of the Confederation. New York also had extensive claims to the west, resting on the colony's traditional relationship with the Six Nations of the Iroquois Confederacy. At the behest of its own delegates, the New York assembly had just passed an act ceding to Congress the state's furthest claims. If Virginia, with its far more extensive claims, followed New York's lead, the Articles might yet be put into operation.

Madison needed little convincing of the wisdom of this policy. Like other key Virginia leaders—Jefferson, Mason, and his fellow delegate, Joseph Jones—he knew the state could never govern the enormous tracts it claimed. Better to limit its boundaries to an area it could govern in a manner consistent with both republicanism and efficiency. Virginia's leaders were willing to cede everything above the Ohio River, provided that certain unauthorized purchases made by various groups of land speculators before the Revolution were invalidated.

During the summer of 1780, delegates from the major landed stated and Maryland negotiated broad terms for the creation of a national domain. Their report faced no major obstacles: nearly every member saw a national domain as the easiest solution to the Union's financial problems. As soon as the measure was approved in September, Joseph Jones returned to Virginia to lobby for an appropriate act of cession. The assembly complied quickly, but continued wrangling delayed final acceptance of the Virginia cession for another three years. Throughout this period, Madison remained the one member of his delegation who most vigorously defended the conditions Virginia attached to its cession. In the meantime, however, the

Confederation was at last on the path to completion. Maryland ratified in February 1781, and Congress set March 1 as the date when the Articles would take effect.

Madison had by then completed a year's service as Congress. Repeated committee appointments marked his growing influence. One newcomer grumbled that he exhibited "all the self-conceit that is common to youth and inexperience"—but the observer, the eccentric Thomas Rodney, claimed direct communion with God and Julius Caesar, and may have been applying unusual standards. A better mark of Madison's stature was his election to a small committee charged with considering how Congress could carry into execution the powers the Articles formally vested in it.

The delegates' eagerness to see the Confederation ratified did not mean that they were satisfied with its actual provisions. The Articles established a pragmatic division of power between Congress and the states. Congress would make foreign policy and decide major questions of national security, while the states regulated their own domestic affairs—or "internal police." The framers of 1777 assumed that the states would act as the administrative arms of Congress, faithfully carrying out its recommendations and providing much of its revenue. Congress received neither coercive authority nor the power to collect its own taxes. As Madison later observed, these omissions had arisen "from a mistaken confidence that the justice, the good faith, the honor, [and] the sound policy" of the assemblies would be enough to make them do their duty.

The intervening years had exposed an alarming gap between the expectations of 1777 and the experience of war. To many delegates the states' frustrating failure to carry out the reforms of 1779–1780 proved that they were simply neglecting their duty. But the real problem was not that the states were negligent; it was rather that the war had imposed greater burdens than they could handle. Even so, many delegates had already decided that Congress needed more power than the Articles bestowed.

How could the states be made to obey Congress? Madison's committee offered a simple solution: give the Union the power literally to coerce delinquent states into doing their duty, either by marching the Continental army within their borders or by stationing armed ships outside their harbors. That so drastic a remedy could even be considered indicated just how seriously the committee viewed the situation, and how difficult it was to imagine how to make the Confederation work. But Madison was convinced that the proposal was practicable. "The situation of most of the states is such," he reminded Jefferson, "that two or three vessels employed against their trade will make it their interest to yield prompt obedience to all just requisitions on them." A majority of Congress thought otherwise. The states would never ratify such an amendment, and even if they did, any attempt to enforce it would create more problems than it resolved. The committee's report was tabled.

The course of the war rendered this issue of compliance less urgent. In October 1781 Congress learned of the surrender of Lord Cornwallis's army at Yorktown in Virginia. Another year and a half passed before peace finally came to America, but the great victory undercut the urgency that had led Madison and others to believe that a power to coerce the states was the most important amendment the Articles needed.

Discussions of the defects of the Confederation shifted instead to finance. All the delegates agreed that the Union had to be rescued from its near bankruptcy. But the driving force behind these deliberations was Robert Morris, the great Philadelphia merchant whom Congress had appointed its first superintendent of finance in February 1781. The most ambitious and successful of the many revolutionaries who mixed patriotism with business, Morris was then at the peak of a spectacular career whose end would come in debtors' prison.

Morris and Madison were both major architects of American nationalism, but their approaches to politics differed sharply. Political theory and parliamentary debate bored Morris, who regarded most routine congressional business as "damn'd trash." In his new post, however, he sought to promote policies to make Congress financially independent of the states. Morris believed instead that the solution to the Confederation's ailments lay in public finance.

Yet while most delegates applauded his administrative efficiency, many opposed allowing Morris to frame policy. Well into 1782, Morris was unable to get Congress to act on the four major elements of his program: a general settlement of accounts among Congress, the states, and private creditors; the assignment to the states of responsibility for satisfying the claims of private creditors; the consolidation of certain other obligations as a *national* debt; and, finally, the grant to the Union of certain fixed revenues—in the form of land, poll, and excise taxes—with which Congress could discharge this debt and acquire the financial independence it lacked under the Confederation.

Opposition to Morris rested on a volatile mix of personal resentment and political suspicion. Some delegates thought that Morris hoped to make himself master of Congress, and they saw in his program the same kind of schemes that had enabled successive British governments to use public finance to sap Parliament of its independence. Personal enmity also came into play when the abrasive Arthur Lee—an old enemy of Morris—joined the Virginia delegation in 1781. Lee and his allies dogged Morris at every turn, denouncing each proposal he sent to Congress.

The Morris program also faced serious obstacles in the state legislatures. Aware that the coming of peace would allow the states to resist the appeals of Congress, Morris tried to provoke an atmosphere of crisis. He badgered officials in the states, fomented discontent among the public creditors across the country, and even evoked the spectre of a military mutiny if the soldiers' grievances over pay and pensions went unrelieved.

Madison supported the goals of Morris's policies as much as he questioned the motives of his opponents. Yet he also stood apart from the inner circle of Morris's supporters. This group included his assistant, the urbane and cynical Gouverneur Morris; the ambitious Alexander Hamilton, once aide-de-camp to General Washington, now a delegate from New York; the Pennsylvania delegate James Wilson, a Scottish immigrant and brilliant lawyer; and Thomas FitzSimons, an Irish immigrant and Philadelphia merchant. An early mark of Madison's independence had come in May 1781, when he was one of a handful of delegates who voted against the Superintendent's request to have Congress grant a charter of incorporation to the privately financed Bank of North America, whose notes Morris intended to use to provide a stable currency to replace Congress's discredited emissions.

No congressional plan of taxation seemed likely to reconcile the divergent interests of the states. A simple tax on land would not be popular in the South, where the holdings of the dominant planter class ran to thousands of acres. But taxes levied on land under cultivation *plus* the value of the improvements made thereon—as Article 8 of the Confederation required—would antagonize New England farmers, with their intensely developed farms. Other issues were just as troubling. Should taxes be collected by state or federal officials? Should the proceeds be applied to current expenses as well as the debt? Should a plan of taxation even be considered before the Articles had a fair trial in peacetime, or before Congress could begin to sell western lands?

These reservations delayed serious discussion of the Morris program until January 1783, when the arrival of a delegation from the army's main camp at Newburgh, New York, brought matters to a head. Seeking to exploit the soldiers' grievances, Morris at last convinced Congress to take up his plan of general taxation.

In the intense maneuvers that followed, Madison not only took a leading in debate and served on every major committee, he also framed the final compromise of April 18 and drafted the circular address that accompanied its submission to the states. During the opening weeks of debate, he joined Hamilton and Wilson in urging the adoption of a plan of national revenues and in opposing the idea of simply asking the states to assign a portion of their own taxes to Congress. On January 28, he introduced a motion designed to break an impasse over the *collection* of taxes by securing broad agreement on the fundamental purposes of national taxation. In a powerful and rigorously logical speech, Madison reviewed the respective merits of the two alternative modes of taxation. No one could deny that a plan of general taxation would fulfill the basic goals of satisfying public creditors, restoring public credit, and meeting the future needs of Congress. But who could speak so confidently, he asked, about the measures that had been proposed merely to preserve state control over taxation? The states had already demonstrated their unreliability, and their performance was hardly likely to improve now that the war was ending. No plan for state taxation could be tried before a comprehensive settlement of accounts *and* an apportionment of expenses according to the formula in Article 8 of the Confederation had been completed; but these steps could take years. Even then, some states might either delay levying taxes until others had acted or divert to their own use taxes collected for national purposes.

Had logic alone been at issue, Madison might have carried the day. But interest and ideology still reigned. Some members opposed any national taxation on principle. Others insisted on giving Article 8 a fair trial. "After all the projects and discussions which have taken place," Madison complained on February 11, "we seem only to have gone round in circle." The opposing positions in Congress were growing more rigid.

Against this background, Madison went to the home of Thomas FitzSimons, the Philadelphia merchant-delegate, on the evening of February 20. There he found Hamilton and three other guests—Richard Peters of Pennsylvania, Daniel Carroll of Maryland, and Nathaniel Gorham of Massachusetts—all supporters of general revenues. The evening began with Hamilton and Peters describing the situation at Newburgh, where talk of mutiny was reputedly rife, and where, Hamilton added, loyalty to Washington declined daily. Hamilton hoped to use this spectre to prod the General into endorsing the plan of taxes—something that Washington, who rigidly honored the principle of military subordination to civilian authority, would never do—and to convince Congress that only its approval of such a scheme would avert a mutiny.

Given his fondness for bold action and his impatience with halfway gestures, Hamilton may have believed that this scenario would actually work. But his company that evening did not share his illusions. They knew that the fear of mutiny could not move a Congress already resentful of Morris's bullying tactics, and that the states would be even less likely to approve measures adopted under such pressures. Over Hamilton's dissent, the others agreed on "the impossibility of adding to the impost on trade any taxes that would operate equally throughout the States, or be adopted by them." When Congress met the next morning, Madison introduced the proposals that formed the basis of the compromise Congress finally adopted. After first restating the case for general taxes, he admitted that "it would be necessary to limit the call for a general revenue to duties on commerce and to call for the deficiency in the most permanent way that could be reconciled with a revenue established within each state separately and appropriated to the common treasury."

Heated debate followed. But by the end of the day, Madison's position had prevailed. A committee of five was named to prepare a new plan of revenue, and its composition—Madison, FitzSimons, Hamilton, Gorham, and Rutledge—suggested that the other members knew something of the previous evening's deliberations. Within two weeks the committee reported the compromise that Congress approved on April 18. It followed the broad outlines of Madison's speech. Congress would ask the states to grant it an impost to last twenty-five years and to be collected by officials appointed by the states, and to levy additional taxes, of their own choosing, which would be appropriated to national purposes.

Even to attain this compromise was not easy. Into March, Hamilton and Wilson still hoped that developments in the army might conspire in their favor. But when the crisis broke at Newburgh, a single gesture from Washington quickly defused the danger. At a meeting called to discuss the army's grievances, the General asked to read to the assembly a letter from Joseph Jones. Pausing to don his eyeglasses, Washington noted "that he had grown gray in their service, and now found himself growing blind." This one remark, evoking as it did memories of the shared sacrifices that had held the army together, recaptured the consciences of the officers, and assured Washington's continued control of the army whose command he had assumed long ago.

The day after Washington punctured the Newburgh conspiracy, Madison reached his thirty-second birthday. His conduct during these debates had revealed his political maturity. Three years in Congress had given him the skills that men steeped in the Anglo-American parliamentary tradition admired. Sober in temperament and methodical in manner, Madison could never have contemplated so risky a stratagem as Hamilton had entertained. Perhaps he lacked Hamilton's driving vision of America as an emerging power, or the younger man's conviction that the answer to the problems of union lay in the mysteries of public finance. Madison's talent lay elsewhere: in a rigorous political intelligence that enabled him both to maintain the integrity of his own positions but also to recognize when logic had to yield to reality.

The influence he now enjoyed had not come easily. His presence was not commanding: as a speaker, he still struggled to master an inherent shyness. But what he lacked in performance he made up for in substance. His speeches were models of thoughtful argument that combined vigorous advocacy of his own ideas with an exhaustive review of alternative positions. No one who listened to them could avoid viewing the issues as Madison wished them to be seen. Logic alone could not overcome the clashing state interests which asserted themselves ever more strongly as war drew to an end; nor could cool reason dispel the passions that stirred a zealot like Arthur Lee. In 1783, as later, Madison had to settle for less than he sought and less than he believed the public good required. But the ability to shape an agenda and to sense possible lines of compromise set leaders apart from backbenchers. By the spring of 1783, these were talents Madison possessed.

On April 15, Congress ratified the peace treaty that John Jay, Benjamin Franklin, and John Adams had negotiated the previous fall. Exactly eight years earlier, the skirmish at Concord and Lexington had plunged America into war. For James Madison, as for so many others, the experience of revolution had involved far more than a shift in political loyalties. In 1775 he had been a slightly priggish young man of twenty-four, whose family's wealth freed him from hard choices about the direction of his own life. Since then he had found in politics an arena in which he could at last express his talents. By ability and diligence, he had entered the ranks of his state's governing elite, gaining the patronage of such elders as Edmund Pendleton and Joseph Jones, and the friendship of leading members of his own generation, like Jefferson and Edmund Randolph. But Madison was not merely another of the many men whom revolution had lifted from a quiet provincial life onto a large stage. Others who had known the satisfactions and frustrations that politics brought now looked forward to a return to private life and long-neglected affairs. Madison faced a different challenge. Few of his contemporaries shared his single-minded commitment to public life. How to fulfill that commitment with both the war and his term in Congress coming to an end was a question he could not yet answer.

CHAPTER FOUR

Legislator

Homesickness was one ailment that never troubled James Madison. Mary House's boardinghouse had become his second home. There, early in 1783, he deepened his friendship with Thomas Jefferson, whose term as governor had ended under a cloud in June 1781, just as Cornwallis's invasion had thrown Virginia into a panic. Events the next year were even more cruel. Jefferson's wife, Martha, had borne six children during their ten years of marriage; the youngest of the three surviving was only four months old when her mother died in September 1782. From the depths of heartbreak, Jefferson accepted a place on the American peace commission. Now he was in Philadelphia, awaiting passage to Europe—unsuccessfully, it turned out, since peace came before a ship could be found—and perhaps encouraging Madison to give up his own bachelorhood.

For in the spring of 1783, Madison's thoughts turned for the first time to love. Among the other boarders at the house on 5th and Market were William Floyd, a delegate from New York, and his three daughters. The youngest, Catherine, caught Madison's eye and exposed him to the "raillery" of his fellow boarders. Just sixteen, she was half his age, but that hardly diminished his attraction to her—nor perhaps hers to him. For a time Madison's hopes were high; but in mid-summer they were crushed. A dejected Madison informed Jefferson that he had fallen victim "to one of those incidents to which such affairs are liable": Kitty had thrown him over for a medical student. He went on to describe his reaction in greater detail—but later in life, after retrieving this letter from Jefferson, he drew heavy lines of ink to blot out the record of his disappointment.

Madison wrote from Princeton, where Congress had fled in June after an angry crowd of unpaid soldiers had surrounded its meetingplace in Philadelphia. The nostalgia he felt for Princeton was undercut by the embarrassment Congress had suffered and the inadequacy of the new capital. Gone were the comforts of his old lodgings; now he shared not only a room but even a bed with Joseph Jones. With the war won and the revenue plan of 1783 still making the rounds of the states, the agenda of Congress seemed suddenly clear. Madison's last task, before his term expired, was to shepherd Virginia's cession of western lands through Congress. Late in October he rejoined Jefferson in Philadelphia. The two rode on to Annapolis, where Jefferson would attend Congress when it reconvened. Early December found Madison back in Montpelier.

Even after an absence of almost four years, the pleasures of homecoming did not disguise his lack of interest in the routines of plantation life. Madison resumed reading law, but with no more idea of practicing than he had shown a decade earlier. Visitors saw him at meals and the evening card table; in between he was off somewhere reading, or perhaps riding. Disappointed in love, he sought no new attachment. Aware of his continued dependence on his family, he considered acquiring land of his own—but only for purposes of speculation, not the tedium of farming.

Once again politics came to his rescue. In April 1784 the voters of Orange County elected Madison a delegate to the state assembly. In May he left home for the new capital at Richmond. During the next three years, his life fell into a routine. When the assembly met—usually in late fall and early winter, the slack months in the planters' calendar—Madison would be in Richmond. Spring and early summer were spent at Montpelier; but then he would head north, visiting Philadelphia, New York, and other points. Here he could buy books hard to find in Virginia, renew old acquaintances, gather fresh political intelligence, and steel himself for the isolation of Montpelier.

His first journey in 1784 was the most ambitious. Leaving Montpelier in late August, he joined the Marquis de Lafayette, the French nobleman who had fought with Washington, at Baltimore. They traveled together to New York, up the Hudson to Albany, and then west along the Mohawk to Fort Stanwix, where they witnessed the opening of a peace treaty between federal commissioners and the hostile tribes of the Iroquois and visited the nearby village of the Oneida tribe. (Later the county where the tribe lived, a nearby town, and the area's first seminary were named to honor the Virginia traveler who saw central New York before land-hungry Yankees turned its wooded hills into a landscape of grain fields, orchards, and pastures.)

Travel diverted Madison, but he knew that his political future lay in Virginia. His reputation had preceded his return to the assembly. No sooner did he take his seat in May 1784 than his friend Edmund Randolph noted that he was already regarded "as a general of whom much has been preconceived to his advantage." Madison lacked the personal followings and oratorical talents that allowed Patrick Henry and Richard Henry Lee to dominate the House of Delegates. But he provided leadership for those who believed that Virginia should pursue policies that would strengthen the Union, permit the repayment of prewar debts to British merchants, reform the court system, and complete the comprehensive revision of old statutes that a committee composed of Jefferson, George Wythe, and Pendleton had recommended five years earlier. From 1784 to 1786, Madison's advocacy of these causes confirmed Randolph's original prediction of the role he would play. What Randolph could not foresee was the impact that three years of service in the assembly would have on Madison.

In Virginia, as in most states, legislative politics were fluid and unpredictable. Often as many as half the delegates were newly elected; how they would vote became known only as a session progressed. The positions of returning members were rarely cast in iron. Some rallied to the banners of the assembly's great men—but the ground where those banners stood often shifted. No one changed positions more adeptly than Patrick Henry. Henry was lazy, inconsistent, and evasive. But once he set his course, he swept many backbenchers along in his wake. Other leaders also swayed blocs of votes, but none rivaled Henry for influence.

The uncertainty of legislative politics had deeper roots than turnover in membership or the idiosyncrasies of leaders. The model legislator was still a man of independent judgment, not the "tool" of a party. Indeed, the idea that a legislator should be a member of a disciplined party was heresy. *Factions* formed around leaders, and *coalitions* appeared on certain issues; but to say that a legislator was an adherent of a *party* was to accuse him of elevating private interest over public good. Yet durable lines of division were emerging as successive sessions of the assembly grappled with such issues as taxes or the payment of British debts. And as leaders like Henry and Madison took well-defined positions, they forced other members to act more consistently.

In 1784 personality still outweighed party. On his way home from Congress, Madison had visited George Mason, hoping to convince the older man to return to the assembly. But Mason valued his privacy and declined the invitation. It was Henry who had to be courted. Early in the session of May 1784, Madison and Joseph Jones took the great man to the coffeehouse for a quiet chat and found him sympathetic to their plans. Yet if promises came easily from Henry—like many a politician, he hated to say no—getting him to deliver was another matter entirely.

Their cooperation was short-lived. By the end of the session, Madison and Henry stood opposed on three major issues, and the basis for their future antagonism seemed set. Henry approved that part of the April 1783 revenue plan altering the formula for allocating the federal expenses among the states, but when it came to appropriating the state's share of taxes, he insisted on a year's delay. Madison believed that the hastily drafted state constitution of 1776 needed amendment; Henry disagreed. Finally, while Madison hoped to complete the disestablishment of religion in Virginia, Henry supported a bill to enable the state to levy a general tax to support "teachers of the Christian religion."

On this thorny matter of religion, Madison gained his greatest legislative victories. At its fall 1784 session, the assembly approved an act to incorporate the Episcopalian church, while postponing action on the assessment bill to levy taxes to support all teachers of Christianity. Madison and his allies used this delay to organize opposition among Baptists, Methodists, and even Presbyterians. Many of the bill's legislative supporters were defeated for reelection, and petitions bearing over ten thousand signatures were presented to the assembly at its fall 1785 session—a staggering feat of organization for its time.

Madison's role in this controversy was not confined to the legislature. In the summer of 1785 he published, anonymously, a *Memorial and Remonstrance against Religious Assessments*. In this short tract, Madison restated the liberal principles he had held since his youth. A tax in support of religion was improper, he argued, because it violated rights of conscience and rested on the "arrogant pretension" that "the civil magistrate is a competent judge of religious truth." But to such familiar themes of the Enlightenment, Madison added new observations that bore the *political* imprint of the Revolution. If the assembly enacted this tax, he argued, it would "overleap the great barrier which defends the rights of the people." Good citizens should thus exercise the same "prudent jealousy" of power they had exhibited before independence. The drift toward the reestablishment of religion would tarnish the state's reputation as "an Asylum to the persecuted and oppressed of every nation and religion" while also "degrad[ing] from the equal rank of citizens all those whose opinions in religion do not bend to those of the legislative authority." It would "destroy that moderation and harmony" among sects that set America apart from other nations, where "torrents of blood have been spilt" in the name of religion. The attempt to enforce a law "obnoxious to so great a proportion of citizens" would only weaken obedience to law in general, particularly if the act were approved "without the clearest evidence that it is called for by a majority of citizens."

Madison's memorial was not the only one to circulate among the state's dissenters, nor was it even the most influential. It is remarkable nevertheless. In treating the establishment of religion as an attack on the liberty and equality of the citizen as well as a violation of the rights of conscience, Madison revealed just how pervasive the language of republicanism had become. Majority rule, the limits of legislative power, the need for a vigilant citizenry: these were all republican principles. But the *Memorial* had a further political facet. It revealed Madison's growing awareness of the importance of public opinion, and of the possibility that sober ideas, carefully presented, could influence voters as well as legislators. If legislators acted improperly, one might appeal over their heads to the constituents whose interests and wishes republican government was meant to represent.

By the time the new assembly convened in October 1785, the general assessment bill was effectively dead. With Henry safely isolated in the governorship—an office that satisfied his vanity and his laziness—Madison looked ahead to the new session with optimism. His principal goal was to push for the wholesale enactment of the revised legislative code which Jefferson—now the American minister to France—had labored so long to prepare. As soon as the assembly met, Madison moved the adoption of the one hundred eighteen bills that made up the code.

The reaction against the assessment bill greatly eased the passage of the one measure that Jefferson and Madison valued most highly: the Act for Establishing Religious Freedom. Though some delegates disliked its language, the bill sailed smoothly through the assembly with only modest changes. In its bold claims for liberty of thought and religious freedom, the Act stands as one of the great monuments of the American Enlightenment. Its ringing preamble condemning every effort to enforce uniformity of religious opinion introduced a second clause affirming absolute rights of conscience and a third paragraph that declared that while the Act was legally revocable, its repeal would be "an infringement of natural right." With justifiable pride, Madison informed Jefferson that its passage had "extinguished for ever the ambitious hope of making laws for the human mind."

Had Madison enjoyed equal success with other bills, his views of state politics might have evolved differently. His careful promotion of the revised code during the early weeks of the session led one member to claim that Madison had "by means perfectly constitutional become almost a dictator upon all subjects that the House have not so far prejudged." But by mid-December 1785, his influence was waning. The amount of work the revised code required was more than most members were prepared to expend. The whole project "might have been finished . . . with great ease," Madison complained, "if the time spent on motions to put it off and other dilatory artifices, had been employed on its merits." But legislative inertia was a fact of life, and Madison had reason to hope that future sessions would approve more than the thirty-six bills adopted when discussion ceased.

More troubling was the opposition mounted against several particularly important bills. The assembly's patience with revision had broken when it deferred to the next session a bill to make punishment fit the severity of the crime—a cherished reform of the Enlightenment. The proposal lost by a single vote, largely because some legislators opposed reducing horse rustling to a non-capital offense. Some crimes were simply too heinous to forgive. Madison's effort to reform the state's judiciary by creating a new set of circuit courts to break the logjam in the existing county courts also fell victim to the legislative maneuvers of its opponents.

By the time the assembly adjourned in late January 1786, Madison had acquired a dose of political humility. The same friend who had hailed his earlier victories now ruefully noted that the best way to get a "favorite scheme" passed was "to get Madison to oppose it." His ever-earnest and reasoned approach to politics grated on his colleagues. Yet those same traits also braced him against disappointment. At the close of the session he sent Jefferson a balanced, even optimistic, appraisal of what had been accomplished and what remained to be done.

National affairs concerned Madison more deeply in the spring of 1786. There would always be a Virginia, he might have reasoned; the survival of the United States was far less certain.

Had Article 5 of the Confederation not barred delegates from serving more than three years of every six, Madison would have preferred to remain in Congress. His interest in its business did not slacken with his return to Virginia; no one in the state was better informed about national politics. At first his major source of intelligence was Jefferson. After Jefferson sailed for France, he corresponded with James Monroe, who had succeeded him in the Virginia delegation as later he would follow Madison as secretary of state and President. Similar views about politics created a friendship that lasted nearly half a century, interrupted only by occasional political rivalry.

In fact, Madison served the Union far more effectively in the assembly than he could possibly have done in Congress. What Congress most needed during the mid-1780s was the support of influential leaders within the states. As a legislator, Madison struggled to persuade his colleagues to approve the various recommendations and requisitions they received from Congress. When by 1786 those efforts had clearly failed, further attempts to reform the Articles had to arise outside of Congress. It was from the Virginia assembly that Madison launched the maneuvers that led to the Annapolis and Philadelphia conventions.

As Madison and other critics of the Articles began to think about the problems of the Union, their first concern was to free Congress from its reliance on the states. Their major priorities were to persuade the states to adopt the revenue plan of April 1783, to comply with other requests for funds, and to complete the land cessions that would finally permit the creation of a national domain. Until Congress escaped its near bankruptcy, other proposals to enhance its authority seemed pointless.

Finances were only the most conspicuous of its problems, however. In addition to capital, Congress needed a capitol. From Princeton, Congress wandered to Annapolis and Trenton before finally settling at New York—a better hunting ground for its many bachelors. Repeated efforts to establish a permanent capital stumbled over the emptiness of the national treasury and the rivalries of states and sections.

More ominous expressions of the danger of sectionalism soon arose in the realm of foreign affairs. With independence won, there was no longer any one overriding national interest to command the ready loyalty of the new republic's three principal regions. Moreover, Congress's inability to frame and implement acceptable policies in this central field of responsibility revealed just how tenuous its authority had become.

The challenge to national interest and congressional power appeared in three distinct issues. The Treaty of Paris called for the repayment of prewar debts and allowed British subjects and American loyalists to sue for the recovery of property confiscated during the war. When the states balked at enforcing these provisions, Britain made their actions a pretext for retaining control of its forts on the Great Lakes. From there the British used their influence over the hostile tribes along the frontier to threaten American expansion above the Ohio River.

Britain also closed West Indian ports to American ships. The West Indian trade had been a vital part of colonial commerce, and American merchants were anxious to regain access to this market. At the same time, British goods carried in British ships flooded America, where consumers were anxious to buy all those favorite items that war had denied them. For many merchants and artisans in northern cities, these actions jeopardized the prosperity that peace was supposed to restore.

A third threat to American interests emerged in 1784, when Spain announced that American goods could not be shipped down the Mississippi River past New Orleans and on to the Gulf of Mexico. Southern leaders feared this action would discourage migrations westward or spur settlers already spilling into Kentucky and Tennessee to separate from the Union. When John Jay, the secretary for foreign affairs, recommended conceding the navigation of the Mississippi in order to complete a commercial treaty with Spain, southern delegates protested that he was sacrificing the expansionist interests of their states to the profits of northern merchants.

Madison viewed all of these issues seriously. In taking on the role of spokesman for the national interest, he hoped to persuade other legislators that the measures Congress had urged them to adopt were reasonable. Often this meant struggling against the interests and prejudices of his colleagues and constituents. No state owed greater debts to British merchants than Virginia; its first reaction to the treaty of peace had been to close its courts to suits by British creditors. Madison repeatedly urged the repeal of this measure; but after coming close to success in 1784, later sessions brought rebuffs.

The difficulties Madison met in these campaigns made him wonder how much could be expected of legislators who were "unaccustomed to consider the interests of the state as they are interwoven with those of the confederacy." "Nothing seems to be more difficult under our new Governments," he wrote Monroe, "than to impress on the attention of our legislatures a due sense of those duties which spring from our relation to foreign nations." Yet with the war over, appeals to a higher patriotism lost their force. He could only hope that time, reason, and events would bring Americans to a true sense of their interest.

Accordingly, during the first three years of peace, Madison favored a strategy of gradual reform. In addition to adopting the revenue plan of 1783, he hoped the states would ratify two modest amendments granting Congress limited power to regulate foreign trade. By the summer of 1785, he was prepared to go one step further. A deepening commercial depression had led Monroe to support an amendment giving Congress general power to regulate both foreign and interstate trade. Within Congress this proposal met such strong opposition that it was not acted upon, but in Virginia, Madison believed that the value of vesting this power in Congress "appears to me not to admit of a doubt."

By August 1785, he deeply feared the costs of inaction. A powerless Congress could not endure indefinitely, Madison knew, nor could the Union itself survive if key interests of different states and regions went unprotected. Should southern opposition prevent northern commercial interests "from obtaining relief by federal means," Madison confessed, "I own, I tremble at the anti-federal expedients into which [they] may be tempted." A northern insistence that a commercial treaty with Spain take precedence over the opening of the Mississippi could prove similarly provocative to the South.

A strategy even of gradual reform required taking a first step. When that step was still not taken after two and a half years of peace, Madison began to consider other alternatives.

At the fall 1785 session of the assembly, Madison supported a resolution to grant Congress broad power to regulate trade. This measure was so whittled down in debate that he preferred to see it die rather than vest Congress with the limited authority the assembly would surrender. But on the verge of adjournment, John Tyler proposed calling an interstate conference to frame an amendment authorizing Congress to regulate American commerce. In the frenzied rush with which legislatures always end their sessions, the members endorsed the idea of inviting the other states to attend this convention and appointed a commission to represent Virginia. Madison, predictably, was one of its members. In March 1786, the Virginia commissioners set the meeting for Annapolis in early September.

At first Madison viewed the idea of a convention with little enthusiasm. Other men—notably Hamilton—had been talking about calling a general convention to amend the Articles since at least 1782, but the cautious Madison thought this idea stood little chance of success. Now he changed his mind. When Monroe objected that the Annapolis agenda was too limited, Madison replied that the friends of the Union could not afford to delay indefinitely. The states now seemed likely to reject any amendment proposed by Congress, he noted; but if the convention could produce a single victory on the issue of commerce, that precedent could "be repeated as other defects force themselves on the public attention, and as the public mind becomes prepared for further remedies." By May 1786, he believed that it would "be best on the whole to suspend measures for a more thorough cure of our federal system, till the partial experiment shall have been made."

In late June Madison took his annual trip north. In New York and Philadelphia he learned that "Many gentlemen both within and without Congress" hoped the Annapolis meeting would lead to "a plenipotentiary convention for amending the confederation." No one would have welcomed such an event more eagerly than Madison, but he still feared that even the modest agenda for Annapolis was more than the public or the state legislatures would accept.

The results at Annapolis came close to anticlimax. Although nine states had accepted Virginia's invitation, only twelve delegates from five states appeared at the appointed time. Even had they waited for a few stragglers known to be en route to arrive, the meeting could clearly not proceed with its task. Yet the Annapolis Convention was poorly attended in numbers only. The dozen commissioners included not only Madison, Hamilton, and John Dickinson, but also Tench Coxe, a close student of American commerce; Abraham Clark of New Jersey and Egbert Benson of New York, two seasoned political leaders; and Madison's two prominent Virginia contemporaries, Edmund Randolph and St. George Tucker.

Rather than adjourn empty handed, these twelve men chose to make the best of the situation. Seizing on a clause in the New Jersey commission suggesting that the convention should range beyond commercial matters, they adopted a report calling on the states to appoint new delegates to attend a general meeting in Philadelphia in May. Its purpose would be nothing less than "to devise such further provisions as shall appear to them necessary to render the constitution of the Federal Government adequate to the exigencies of the Union." The commissioners stopped short of describing the proposed meeting as a constitutional convention, but it took little imagination to sense what they had in mind. It was at once a bold and desperate move. The commissioners hoped that their call would galvanize public opinion, but they feared even more strongly the consequences of inaction. Every other scheme to strengthen the Union had failed.

Before Annapolis, Madison's pessimism had led him to err on the side of caution; now, in a curious way, it convinced him that the moment for risk taking had come. He no longer assumed that time favored the cause of reform. The possibility that the nation might dissolve into two or three regional confederacies seemed ever more plausible. Madison knew that months of quarreling over John Jay's negotiations with the Spanish minister Gardoqui had split Congress into two starkly sectional factions. A Union that already lacked the means to enforce its will would be hard pressed to weather prolonged disagreements over basic policies.

Madison returned to Virginia in October, accompanied on his journey by Monroe and his new bride. On the way they stopped at Mount Vernon to visit George Washington. Madison knew the General would support the coming convention, but he wanted something more from Washington: a commitment to attend the meeting in person and thereby lend his immense prestige to the cause of reform. His courtship of Washington was not the least important task Madison set for himself in preparing for the meeting at Philadelphia.

Late October found Madison in Richmond for the fall session of the assembly. His first concern was to secure approval for the Annapolis report and the appointment of a delegation for the meeting at Philadelphia. Prompt action by Virginia was vital not only because it had sponsored the Annapolis meeting but also because the commissioners had *officially* transmitted their report only to the states, not to Congress.

Madison feared that resentment over the Mississippi issue might prejudice many legislators against any plan to strengthen the Union in general. He was accordingly pleased when the bill he drafted sailed unopposed through the assembly. "The evidence of dangerous defects in the Confederation," he told Jefferson, "has at length proselyted the most obstinate adversaries to a reform." He was equally pleased with the weighty delegation the assembly then appointed. Besides Madison, it included Governor Edmund Randolph, George Wythe, George Mason, Patrick Henry—and George Washington, whom Madison had nominated in the hope that duty would ultimately triumph over convenience. Only Henry refused the nomination—"I smelled a rat," the wily old leader supposedly claimed later—but Madison knew the selection of so powerful a delegation would impress legislators in other states.

His own reelection to Congress was also gratifying. Still fearful that a wrong turn in the Spanish negotiations could upset everything, Madison was anxious to return to Congress to prevent John Jay's diplomacy from provoking a sectional crisis. When the assembly adjourned in January, Madison stopped at Montpelier for three days and then set off northward, stopping again to consult General Washington. He reached New York on February 11, 1787, after "a very tedious journey" whose final leg carried him into the teeth of a northeastern blizzard.

A bitter winter had also delayed his first trip to Congress in 1780, and it would be surprising if Madison did not think back on all that had happened since. He had more than fulfilled the expectations that had led his state's leaders to appoint an overly earnest but intelligent and disciplined young man to the thankless position of delegate to Congress. A month shy of his thirty-sixth birthday, he had now become a major figure in state and national politics. More than that, he had reached a stage in life where he could direct his talents toward the achievement of one paramount aim. On the eve of the Convention, experience left him as well prepared as any of the fifty-five men who would join in framing the Constitution. He had become a keen judge of men and measures in his understanding of how to court a Washington or neutralize a Henry, in his grasp of the nuances of legislative politics, and in his calculations of the tactical problems of promoting an interstate movement to reform the confederation. Yet in the end, among a generation of leaders well steeped in the literature of political theory, his greatest contributions to the founding of the republic flowed from the force of his intellect.

CHAPTER FIVE

Extending the Republic

James Madison went to the Constitutional Convention of 1787 intent on seizing the initiative from the opening moments. But the proposals he carried with him represented far more than a list of his own priorities. They amounted to a comprehensive theory of government that consciously challenged many axioms of eighteenth-century political science. Madison came to the Convention in the grip of a deep intellectual passion, convinced that he had diagnosed the faults not just of the Confederation but also of the republican constitutions of the states.

The best-known statements of Madison's ideas appear in *The Federalist*—the series of eighty-five essays that he, Alexander Hamilton, and John Jay later wrote to support the ratification of the Constitution. But the mature views expressed in such famous essays as the Tenth and Fifty-first *Federalist* have to be set against the private papers that Madison drafted *before* the Convention, which offer a far more revealing insight into his thoughts and plans. Here he not only traced the problems of the Union to the "vicious" character of the state governments, but also explained how the revision of the Confederation could cure the mischief of popular government within the states. Reviewing the history of the states since independence, he drew important lessons for the reconstruction of the national government. At the same time, he also came to believe that only the creation of an effective national government would rescue the states from their own failings.

At the heart of Madison's thinking lay a deep concern with the process by which laws were enacted, enforced, and obeyed, and an overriding conviction that the legislatures created by the state constitutions of 1776 had failed to discharge their duties fairly or responsibly. This concern grew naturally from the frustrations Madison had felt in each of the offices he had held since 1778. As a member of the Virginia council, he had learned how difficult it was to execute laws rashly made or vaguely worded. As a delegate to Congress, he had seen individual states balk at carrying out measures necessary for the common good. And as a member of the Virginia assembly, he had concluded that most legislators ordinarily acted on short-sighted calculations of their own interests or those of their constituents.

Madison traced these problems to the design of the state constitutions, most of which had effectively concentrated all powers of government in the legislatures. The constitution writers of 1776 had looked backward to the abuses of power the colonists had suffered at the hands of royal governors. This history had led them to transfer power to popularly elected assemblies, but events since 1776 had revealed that inexperienced legislators confronting the staggering problems the war created, and subject to intense pressures from their constituents, could not act with the "*wisdom* and steadiness" the situation required. This effective concentration of power in the assemblies had left the executive and judicial branches of government unable either to assist in lawmaking or to resist improper legislative interference with their own duties. Only the constitutions adopted by New York in 1777 and Massachusetts in 1780—after some lessons of war had been learned—restored a measure of the powers that the colonial governors had previously enjoyed.

How could these problems be remedied? Madison first pondered this question in August 1785, when a college friend solicited his advice about the kind of constitution Kentucky might adopt should it be separated from Virginia. In reply, Madison emphasized the peculiar value of an upper house (or senate) composed of a small number of members serving long terms of office on fixed salaries—conditions that would leave them independent of both their electors and their colleagues in the lower house. Such a body, in Madison's scheme, was not meant to represent anything, but simply to check the lower house by preventing the adoption of poorly framed laws. As a further aid to the task of legislation, Madison proposed the appointment of a select committee of members possessing the actual skills needed to draft bills correctly—men like George Mason or George Wythe (or Madison himself).

Madison originally believed that resistance to improper laws had to arise within the legislature itself. Neither the executive nor the judiciary, he thought, would be politically strong enough to challenge a legislature claiming to speak for the community at large. Rather than give the governor a veto over state laws, or authorize the judiciary to declare laws unconstitutional, he sought instead to guarantee the independence of the other two branches of government.

Before Madison could apply these insights to the problems of the Union, he had to perceive how the issues of republicanism and federalism could be fused. This process began to unfold in the winter of 1786, when he read widely in the history of "Ancient and Modern Confederacies." His notes from these studies reveal his concern with the great problem all confederations face: how to maintain the authority of a central government against the claims of its member states. But the great breakthrough in his thinking occurred only during the months preceding the Convention. In his leisure hours as a member of Congress, Madison directed his thoughts to the American situation.

The fruit of this labor was a memorandum on "the vices of the political system of the United States"—one of those rare documents in the history of political theory in which one can literally observe an original thinker forge his major discovery. In its opening pages, Madison reviewed the familiar criticisms of the Confederation: the refusal of the states to honor the requisitions of Congress or to respect its authority, notably in foreign affairs; their inability to deal fairly with one another or to agree on measures vital to the common interest; and, above all, the failure of the framers of the Articles to recognize that the resolutions of Congress had to rest on the same coercive powers that gave force to all ordinary acts of government.

With these points detailed, however, he took up another set of issues. "In developing the evils which viciate the political system of the U.S.," he wrote, "it is proper to include those which are found within the states individually, as well as those which affect the states collectively, since the former class have an indirect influence on the general malady and must not be overlooked in forming a complete remedy." Here, quietly but powerfully, the ground of his thought had shifted, away from the weaknesses of the Union and toward the problems of the states. There the "multiplicity," "mutability," and "injustice" of the laws passed since independence has called "into question the fundamental principle of republican government, that the majority who rule in such governments, are the safest guardians both of public good and private rights." It would not be enough for the Convention simply to propose additional powers for Congress, Madison implied. It would also have to ask how the reform of the Articles could remedy the "vicious legislation" that had sullied the republican cause within the states.

The simple truth, Madison believed, was that incompetent legislators were passing too many laws, and these poorly drawn acts were being repealed or revised before anyone could discover how well they were actually working. Such proceedings brought the very concept of law into contempt. In a republic obedience to law rested neither on the efficiency of monarchy or on the influence of an able aristocracy but on the free compliance of citizens who believed that the laws were rightly made and fairly executed. Call that faith into question, Madison understood, and the willingness to abide by law would crumble.

Nor did he limit his concern to the mere ineptitude of the assemblies. What seemed "still more alarming" was the passage of laws that were not only unwise but *unjust*. Particularly troubling were acts violating the private rights of individuals, such as the Rhode Island laws that made a depreciating paper currency legal tender for the payment of debts. Republics were customarily regarded as the form of government best designed to protect both individual liberties and the general rights of the people against the power of the state or the designs of ambitious rulers. But because republics demanded so much of their people, they were also the most fragile forms of government. Fearful of trusting human nature too far, previous writers on government had argued that stable republics could only survive in small and relatively homogeneous societies, where the similarity of interests would reduce the temptation one part of the community might feel to exploit another. They further argued that a republican people had to be virtuous, by which they meant that citizens had to be willing to subordinate private interests to public good.

Americans in 1776 had concluded that their society met these conditions. True, the new nation covered an enormous expanse of territory—but one conveniently divided into thirteen autonomous states. Social distances also seemed narrow. There was no titled aristocracy, no large cities, and no starving peasantry—and it was easy enough to ignore half a million slaves who lacked any political existence. Most Americans farmed modest plots; most possessed the independent livelihood that republican theorists also demanded of citizens. And their very acts of resistance had revealed the Americans to be an unusually virtuous people.

What, then, was to be done? In his analysis, Madison sought to demonstrate how an entirely different set of assumptions could reaffirm the American commitment to republican government. In so doing, however, his deepest concern was to prove that a national republic would protect minority interests and individual rights against the danger of a "factious majority": a majority which, while claiming to embody the popular will, actually preferred its own interests to the public good.

It was futile, he argued, to expect restraint from ordinary legislators who typically sought office for ambition and self-interest. Even honest lawmakers could not always see through the "sophistical arguments" of "a favorite leader" (a Patrick Henry, for example). Even less faith could be placed in the people at large. Experience taught that neither "a prudent regard" for the general good nor "respect for character" nor even religion could deter an impassioned or interested majority from pursuing "unjust violations of the rights and interests of the minority, or of individuals." For, as Madison noted, "All civilized societies are divided into different interests and factions as they happen to be creditors or debtors—rich or poor—husbandmen, merchants or manufacturers—members of different religious sects—followers of different political leaders—inhabitants of different districts—owners of different kinds of property etc."

The idea that modern societies were made up of different interests was a commonplace of eighteenth-century thought. The novelty of Madison's theory lay in his use of this self-evident description of society to undermine some of the classic axioms of republican thought. No society, Madison understood, could attain the homogeneity and uniformity that previous writers demanded of republics; nor could any population divided along so many lines and subject to all the impulses and failings of human nature long expect to operate on virtue alone. Even the smallest society—Rhode Island, for example—was prone to divisions, Madison reasoned; but more than that, the danger to liberty would be far greater there than in a larger, more complex society. In a small republic, "the impulse of a common interest or passion" would sweep through the population easily. But the task of forming coherent, durable factions would prove far more difficult in a large republic. Even though its citizens were *individually* just as likely to feel the same selfish motives, such a society would be "broken into a greater variety of interests, of pursuits, of passions, which check each other, whilst those who feel a common sentiment have less opportunity of communication and concert."

Madison had thus proved both that a republic need not rest on unrealistic expectations of human nature and that a national government could protect individual liberty more readily than an individual state. But he also believe that "an enlargment of the sphere" would have an "auxiliary" benefit. It would permit such "a process of elections as will most certainly extract from the mass of the society the purest and noblest characters which it contains." The virtue the people lacked might yet appear among their representatives. If elections were held in large districts, the local demagogues who dominated state politics would cancel each other out, clearing the field for persons of genuine merit and reputation to rise to the national legislature. There they would frame laws based not on narrow calculations of local interest but on enlightened notions of true public good.

In reaching these conclusions, Madison relied upon the Scottish philosopher and historian, David Hume, whose essay on the "Idea of a Perfect Commonwealth" made a similar argument. Yet the intellectual debt Madison owed to Hume does not lessen the originality of his achievement. That a speculative essay could so inspire him is a mark of his ability to apply bookish learning to real problems. But his perception of the "vices of the political system" was rooted far more deeply in the frustrations he had encountered in both state and national politics.

Equally important, the general argument for the extended republic could define neither the agenda that Madison wanted the Convention to follow nor the specific proposals he wished it to adopt. Proud as he was of his intellectual achievement, he did not regard himself as one of those "ingenious theorists" whose best thinking occurred "in his closet or in his imagination." Instead he was far more intent on the uses to which he hoped to put his ideas at Philadelphia. He spelled out his own agenda in letters to Jefferson, Edmund Randolph, and Washington.

His fundamental concern was to find some "middle ground" between the current confederation, in which the states effectively held sovereignty, and "a consolidation of the whole into one simple republic." Since experience revealed that the states could not be counted upon to execute acts of Congress faithfully, Madison proposed to allow the new government to act directly upon the population, bypassing the state governments entirely. Depriving the states of their federal functions would have the further advantage of undercutting their claim to equal representation in Congress: states need no longer be represented as states. Representation could instead be apportioned among them on the basis of their population or wealth (or both). And because the legislative powers the Union required were so substantial—and thus potentially dangerous to liberty—the new Congress would also need two houses.

The key to Madison's position and to his strategy at the Convention was to insist that representation in *both* houses had to rest upon some scheme of apportionment. His unwillingness to compromise on this issue stemmed in part from a pragmatic calculation. Without such a change, he feared, the most populous states would reject any significant revision of the Articles, especially in the vital areas of taxation and commerce. In the end, the small states would simply have to yield and accept their inferiority. But Madison's rigidity had one further source. In 1787, as in 1785, he still believed that in a republic the legislature must ever remain the dominant institution. Though recognizing that the two weaker branches—the executive and judiciary—deserved protection against legislative interference in their own duties, he doubted whether they could serve as an effective counterweight against the legislature in the task of lawmaking. For this reason, he viewed the upper house of the legislature as the critical institution of any government. A small, carefully selected senate would offer the safest barrier against improper legislation and the best repository for power over war, foreign affairs, and appointments to major offices. But the large states could never accept that kind of senate if it retained the system of equal state voting used by Congress.

Moreover, this concern with the upper house was intimately connected with his condemnation of state legislation. For the overriding conviction that factious majorities *within the states* posed the greatest danger to liberty drove Madison to his most radical conclusion: that the new government should possess "a negative *in all cases whatsoever* on the legislative acts of the States." This veto would extend not simply to state acts that threatened "to invade the national jurisdiction," but also to laws that violated the rights of individuals and minorities. The national government would thus serve as a "disinterested and dispassionate umpire in disputes between different interests and passions" within each of the states, protecting less powerful interests against the excesses of local majorities, and extending its oversight even to "local questions of policy."

This radical power, Madison conceded, was identical with the "kingly prerogative" that the British crown had exercised over its colonies before the Revolution. As he well knew, Jefferson had bitterly denounced the royal veto of colonial legislation in the Declaration of Independence. Nothing more clearly reveals Madison's alarm over the character of state politics than his endorsement of so controversial a proposal—and one so unlikely to be accepted, if not by the Convention, then certainly by the states. What alone justified this unlimited veto was the belief that fundamental rights of property were being rendered insecure by the populist legislation the states seemed increasingly inclined to adopt. The demand for paper money and debtor stay laws frightened him terribly; the time might not be distant, he feared, when assaults on property would go even further. Beyond all the other uses to which it could be put, the veto was Madison's best answer to the danger he foresaw.

Which branch of the national government could exercise this sweeping power most fairly? Aware that a bicameral veto would prove unwieldy, Madison concluded that the power "might be most conveniently exercised" by the upper house of Congress. Two conclusions followed. First, senators elected by state legislatures could hardly be expected to overturn the acts of their constituents. Some other form of election was necessary. Second, the large states would never allow this power to be held by an upper house that retained the rule of equal state voting.

This radical proposal lay at the heart of his conception of the role the national government would play in preserving both the union of the states and the republican form of government. But Madison's attachment to this scheme also sharply narrowed the field of maneuver within which he could act at the Convention. It made the composition of the Senate—both the mode of its election and the apportionment of its members—the critical issue upon which everything else depended.

Convinced that he had found a comprehensive solution to the vices of republican government, Madison went to Philadelphia bent on persuasion, not compromise.

CHAPTER SIX

The Great Convention

None of the fifty-five members of the Federal Convention contributed more to the framing of the Constitution than James Madison. Yet save for the handful of delegates who later opposed its ratification, few members left Philadelphia in September more disappointed with the Constitution than the man history called its "Father." In part this reaction marked the letdown Madison felt after four months of intense deliberations, in part the high expectations he had brought to the Convention. Soon enough Madison put his reservations aside and threw himself into the campaign for ratification. Yet his early disappointment illustrates the special character of the Convention. At one level, the delegates grappled with fundamental principles of government; at another, they struggled to protect the interests of their constituents. Madison hoped an appeal to high principles would overcome parochial loyalties; instead, the play of interests within the Convention forced him to modify his own principles.

Only the rare assembly in eighteenth-century America managed to muster a quorum on time; the Federal Convention proved no exception. Monday, May 14, found only a few delegates present, Madison among them. In fact, he was the first on the scene from any state other than the host. He arrived in Philadelphia on the 5th and immediately took up his old lodgings with Mary House. No doubt he hoped to use this time to refine his own thoughts and to sound out other members as they arrived.

Not until May 25 did the Convention attain a quorum of seven states; but the Virginians were fully present by May 17. Madison knew an opportunity when he saw one. Had the other delegations appeared on time, the Convention would probably have begun with cautious efforts to define common concerns and a plan of action. But with time on their hands, the Virginians decided to seize the initiative. Meeting each afternoon, they drafted a fifteen-point plan of government which they could introduce whenever the Convention was ready to take up "the main business."

Time also allowed the Virginians to consider how they could best convince the small states to relinquish their equal vote in Congress. Conversations with Gouverneur Morris and Robert Morris revealed that some delegates favored an immediate confrontation on this issue; the two Pennsylvanians thought "the large states should unite in firmly refusing to the small States an equal vote" within the Convention itself. But before the rules of procedure were adopted on May 28, the Virginians dissuaded them from risking "fatal altercations" so early. Instead Madison counted on convincing the small states "in the course of the deliberations, to give up their equality for the sake of an effective Government."

Two other Convention rules deserve notice. One came so naturally that it did not even need formal approval: everyone simply assumed they would meet behind closed doors. But the Convention further reinforced this privacy by agreeing that "nothing spoken in the House [shall] be printed, or otherwise published or communicated without leave." Candid debate would be impossible if reports passed beyond the chamber. If disgruntled delegates felt free to alert their constituents to the radical ideas that *other* members proposed, the Convention would quickly reach deadlock. Privately, some delegates came to wish that the secrecy rule could be waived; but their honor as gentlemen bound them to obedience.

Most of what was said at Philadelphia might thus have died with the framers. But Madison was determined that the debates not be lost to history. Recalling the frustration he had met while studying the history of other confederacies, and foreseeing the curiosity later generations would feel about this meeting, he set about the tiresome task of recording what was said. Taking a seat directly in front of Washington, the unanimous choice as presiding officer, he kept a running record of the debates. Yet in taking on this wearying task, Madison was obeying the needs of politics as well as history. His notes enabled him to prepare for the next round of debate, to mark inconsistencies in argument, to temper his own appeals to the flow of discussion. For his entire strategy rested on the assumption that the delegates would be receptive to candid argument and persuasion. And within this extraordinary forum, he meant to see his own ideas and proposals prevail on their merits.

The preparation of the Virginia Plan fit this strategy perfectly. The fifteen articles that Governor Edmund Randolph presented on May 29 were not Madison's work alone. He could not simply impose his ideas on a delegation that included Randolph, Mason, George Wythe, and Washington himself. Yet in almost every respect the Plan conformed to Madison's concerns. First and foremost, it proposed replacing the existing unicameral Congress with a true national government of three independent branches. Representation in the two houses of the legislature would be "proportioned" either to the taxes each state paid into the national treasury, or to its free population. A popularly elected lower house would in turn elect the upper house from candidates nominated by the state legislatures. The executive and some part of the judiciary would form a "council of revision" with a limited veto over both national and state laws; but the new congress would retain the right to override that veto and to pass final judgment on the validity of state laws. Other articles provided for admitting new states into the Union; guaranteed a republican form of government to each state; and proposed procedures both for ratifying and amending the new constitution.

How much power would this government actually exercise? On this vital question, the Virginia Plan spoke in broad but vague terms. The new legislature would enjoy the rights Congress possessed under the Confederation and the authority to act "in all cases to which the separate States are incompetent, or in which the harmony of the United States may be interrupted by the exercise of individual [state] legislation." It would also possess the right to use force against any state "failing to fulfill its duty," and to "negative all [state] laws contravening . . . the articles of Union."

Immediately after Randolph finished presenting the Virginia Plan, the Convention adjourned for the day. The delegates lingered to make copies of the Plan; then they drifted off in small groups to ponder its implications. Privately many were stunned by its sweeping delegation of power, which far exceeded anything seriously discussed during the 1780s. But the central thrust of the Virginia Plan lay elsewhere. Unlike all previous proposals for amending the Confederation, it steered attention away from the *authority* the Union would exercise. It emphasized instead the *structure* of the government and, in particular, the demand of the more populous states for a system of representation that would no longer rest on the absurd idea that Maryland, Rhode Island, and Delaware deserved an equal vote with Virginia, Pennsylvania, and Massachusetts.

All of this followed Madison's calculation that a change in the principle of representation was the decisive first step the Convention had to take before it could determine exactly what the national government would do. In fact, the dispute over representation preoccupied the delegates for seven weeks, until the so-called Great Compromise of July 16 secured the small states an equal vote in the Senate. From the outset the critical test involved the composition of the upper house. In a bicameral legislature, the right of the large states to proportional representation in *one* house could not be denied. The real dispute was whether to apply that principle to *both* houses. A few small state leaders, like crusty Roger Sherman of Connecticut and John Dickinson of Delaware, quickly staked out their own ultimatum, insisting that their states would reject any government that deprived them of an equal vote in at least one house of Congress.

To this position they clung doggedly. In many ways, the small states had the easier task of defending a privilege they already enjoyed. By contrast, the supporters of apportionment had to prove not only that the states as such did not deserve representation, but also that the new government could not operate effectively if the individual legislatures exerted the same influence they enjoyed under the Confederation.

The arguments with which the large state delegates supported these claims were largely the same ones that Madison had prepared before the Convention. His allies did not endorse every facet of his thought. James Wilson of Pennsylvania, Alexander Hamilton of New York, Rufus King of Massachusetts, and Charles Pinckney of South Carolina were powerful thinkers in their own right, and at times their positions and his diverged. But taken together, the arguments and the strategy of the large state delegates followed the approach Madison had pioneered. For his own part, Madison seized every opportunity to eduate the Convention in his new teachings about republican government.

The opening fortnight of debate (May 29–June 13) went nearly as well as Madison could have hoped. Sitting as a committee of the whole, the Convention worked through the Virginia Plan with relative ease. On many points the delegates seemed ready to offer only tentative opinions. When they first took up the executive branch, for example, silence reigned until Benjamin Franklin gently chided his colleagues for their "shyness." But such prodding was not needed on the issue of representation, and here no one spoke more directly than Madison. He put the main point bluntly on May 31, when he declared that "whatever reason might have existed for the equality of suffrage when the Union was a federal one among sovereign States . . . must cease when a national Government" acting directly on the people "should be put into the place." And when Roger Sherman suggested on June 6 that few "objects" would require national attention even under a new constitution, Madison went out of his way to rebut this claim, seizing the occasion to present the Convention with his first summary of the dangers of faction *within* the states.

Such arguments, and the advantage the Virginians had gained by seizing the initiative, brought early votes favorable to the apportionment of representation in both houses, the popular election of the lower chamber, the broad delegation of legislative power the Virginia Plan proposed, and even the national veto. On only one issue did Madison suffer a serious setback, when on June 7 all ten states present voted to permit the state legislatures to elect the members of the upper house. Madison and Wilson opposed this proposal strongly, arguing that the dismal record of the state assemblies justified denying them any direct influence over the appointment of national officers. But Madison saw further dangers lurking in this vote. The idea that one house should represent the state *governments*—rather than population or property—could support a claim for an equal vote. Moreover, the upper house would lose its character as a small, highly select institution even if legislative election and proportional voting were both honored: give Delaware one senator, and Virginia would need sixteen. "Enlarge their number," Madison observed, "and you communicate to them the vices they are meant to correct."

The committee of the whole finished its review of the Virginia Plan on June 13. The next day William Paterson of New Jersey declared that a group of small state delegates needed time to present a plan based on "purely federal" principles. Paterson introduced the New Jersey Plan—as it is called—on Friday the 15th. Once again, the delegates promptly adjourned for the day, taking time only to copy Paterson's nine articles.

Before Madison left the State House, however, an angry John Dickinson took him aside. A man of conciliatory temper, Dickinson had had the thankless task of drafting the first version of the Articles of Confederation a decade earlier. Now he berated Madison for his obstinacy. "You see the consequence of pushing things too far," Dickinson warned. "Some of the members from the small States wish for two branches in the General

Legislature; and are friends to a good National Government; but we would sooner submit to a foreign power than submit to be deprived of an equality of suffrage in both branches of the legislature, and thereby be thrown under the domination of the large states."

In appearance, the New Jersey Plan resembled the limited amendments to the Confederation that both Dickinson and Madison had supported in the mid-1780s. It proposed keeping the existing Congress intact, with states still voting equally, while also establishing a national executive and judiciary. But the actual powers the Union would exercise remained limited. Congress would gain only the authority to regulate commerce and to raise revenue through duties on foreign imports, stamp taxes, and the post office. Moreover, Paterson supposed that Congress would often act through the states rather than directly upon the population.

Like other large state delegates, Madison suspected that the New Jersey Plan was not meant to be taken seriously. Even its supporters did not defend it as an adequate response to national problems: they merely argued that no stronger government could be formed if the smaller states lost the security of an equal vote in one house of the legislature. But precisely because the friends of the New Jersey Plan had so little to defend, its foes saw much to attack. On June 16, Wilson and Randolph led the offensive, arguing that the Convention was not confined to considering mere amendments to the Confederation, but could propose whatever seemed necessary. When the delegates reassembled on Monday the 18th, Alexander Hamilton held the floor all day while giving his famous speech expressing admiration for the British constitution and calling for a government far more potent than even the Virginia Plan envisioned.

Hamilton's speech, all agreed, was intellectually impressive but politically irrelevant. It fell to Madison to deliver the final blow against the New Jersey Plan. Point by point, his speech of June 19 summarized his earlier analysis of the vices of the political system. Taking Paterson's plan at face value, he used it as a foil to restate all the reasons why a mere revision of the Confederation would fail, and also to remind the delegates that their work should extend to the internal problems of the states. But Madison was equally careful to bring his colleagues back to the major issue. "The great difficulty lies in the affair of Representation," he concluded; "and if this could be adjusted, all others would be surmountable."

When he finished speaking, there was literally nothing left to say, and the Convention immediately went on to reject the New Jersey Plan by a vote of seven states to three, with Maryland divided. But in a curious way, the real debate over the New Jersey Plan began only *after* its rejection. For representation *was* the crucial issue, as Madison had rightly noted and always insisted, and no progress could be made on anything else until this single question was resolved.

The trying time of the Convention came during the four weeks of debate that followed (June 20–July 16). The challenge Madison and his allies faced was to convert the margin of their victory of June 19 into a stable coalition favoring proportional representation in both houses. But if they hoped the opposition would yield gracefully, disappointment came quickly. Rather than abandon the field, the small state bloc offered a series of amendments designed to build their case for the "compromise" they sought. It mattered little that these motions stood no chance of success: each time the small states *lost* a vote, their pleas for compromise gained new weight. Equally important, these votes provided a continuing test of the two parties' strength and will. When the last amendment, calling for an equal state vote in the Senate, failed by a tie vote of five states on July 2, the Convention faced deadlock—and deadlock, in turn, reinforced the call for compromise.

Throughout this period, Madison, Wilson, King, and Hamilton subjected their opponents to withering arguments. How could the three most populous states ever find common motives for violating the rights and interests of the small states, Madison asked on June 28? In their manners, religion, history, and economies, "they could not have been more effectually separated from each other by the most jealous citizen of the most jealous State." Would mere size alone ever provide a common basis for action? The large states were far more likely to view each other as rivals than fellow conspirators. How could the states even claim a right of representation, Madison asked? He defied anyone to name "a single instance in which the General Government was not to operate on the people individually." Equally important, the history of all confederacies—including the American—proved that the greater danger to the public good came from the "encroachments" the individual parts made on the whole: give the state governments a direct voice in legislation, and they would prevent the national government from acting.

These were powerful arguments, and with them Madison and his colleagues repeatedly battered their opponents—only to see the small states' spokesmen hold their ground. Sensing the advantage slipping away, Madison injected a new argument into the debate. "The great division of interests in the United States," he noted on June 29, "did not lie between the large and small States: It lay between the Northern and Southern, and if any defensive power were necessary, it ought to be given to these two interests." Apportion seats in one house according to free population only, Madison suggested, and in the other house by free population plus three-fifths of the slaves: then a balance between sections would be struck.

But Madison balked at turning this hint into a formal motion. The intellectual advantage to be gained by invoking the potential for sectional conflict did not outweigh its risks. True, sectional differences rooted in slavery would endure long after the Convention adjourned—which could not be said of the dispute between small and large states. But by emphasizing the stark difference between North and South, Madison came close to contradicting his own theory that an extended republic would protect liberty by multiplying the number of interests it embraced. Moreover, if the protection of broad interests became the rule of apportionment, how could Madison justify granting the legislature the unrestricted veto he believed it required? How could the South ever accept a national veto over laws affecting slavery?

Even when the tie vote of July 2 revealed that deadlock was at hand, Madison hoped to resolve the critical question through debate on the Convention floor. But a majority of members felt otherwise. After spirited discussion, a committee of one member from each state was elected "to devise and report some compromise" on the entire issue of representation. And the delegates indicated just which direction they hoped the committee would take in choosing its members. The three largest states were represented by George Mason, Benjamin Franklin, and Elbridge Gerry, each of whom had already indicated his willingness to work for compromise and conciliation.

The committee met on July 3, joined the other delegates in celebrating the eleventh anniversary of independence the next day, and delivered its report on the 5th. Madison could not accept the compromise that the committee unenthusiastically proposed. In exchange for giving the small states an equal vote in the Senate, the large states would receive the assurance that revenue and appropriation bills would originate in the lower house and not be "altered or amended" by the Senate. Madison immediately denied that "any concession on the side of the small states" had been offered. The Senate had no need to alter a bill it disliked: it could simply reject it until the lower house sent the measure back up in "the desired shape."

But the fact that this measure was offered as a compromise changed the very terms of debate. Many delegates were tired of weighing the large states' appeal for justice against the small states' demand for security; now they could simply ask whether the success of the Convention depended on compromise itself. The debate that led up to the decision of July 16 accordingly avoided the central issue of the equal state vote. Instead it focused on the apportionment of seats in the lower house of Congress alone. Here conflict over whether slaves should be counted for purposes of representation revealed, as Madison had foreseen, that sectional differences posed the greatest threat to the Union. Again Madison sought to use the reality of sectional differences to expose the weakness of claims based only on the size of the state—but to no avail.

In their final speeches of Saturday, July 14, Madison, King, and Wilson restated their major arguments. Belatedly, they even proposed a modest compromise to modify the distribution of seats in the Senate so that Virginia, the largest state, would have only five votes, while Delaware and absent Rhode Island would each have one. But the small state leaders, sensing victory, would not bargain. When the Convention reassembled on Monday, it accepted the committee's report, five states to four, with Massachusetts divided.

Defeat temporarily left the large state leaders too stunned to continue. Rather than have the Convention promptly move on to the next issue, Randolph asked for an adjournment, so "that the large States might consider the steps proper to be taken in the present solemn crisis of the business, and that the small States might also deliberate on the means of conciliation." But the large state delegates who caucused the next morning were unable to decide on any plan of action. "The time was wasted in vague conversation," Madison noted, and from this point on the small state leaders knew that their key demand was secure.

Discouraged as Madison was by the decision of the 16th and the disarray of his allies, he grew more upset as the Convention went on to reject two other proposals to which he was deeply committed. He still thought that unchecked legislatures posed the greatest threats to the constitution of any republic. Against the danger that state lawmaking would continue to jeopardize both national interests and private rights, he remained attached to the idea of the national veto. And against the fallibility of the national legislature, he proposed the creation of a council of revision, composed of both the executive and members of the judiciary, who could advise the lawmakers about pending bills while backing their advice with the threat of a veto.

These were the two critical proposals that the Convention went on to reject during the week of July 16. The first to go was the pet scheme of a national veto on state laws, eliminated by a vote of seven states to three on the 17th. In its place, the Convention accepted a seemingly weaker resolution simply stating that national laws and treaties were to be "the supreme law" of the states. Four days later, on Saturday the 21st, Madison and Wilson mounted a last effort to convince the Convention to accept the council of revision. Here, too, they met failure. The great objection they could not overcome held that it was improper to involve the judges in the task of legislating. Most members seemed to assume that judges would act more effectively simply by declaring laws violating the constitution void—through what would soon be known as the power of judicial review.

To sustain three such defeats in the space of a week must have devastated the Madison who had come to Philadelphia imbued with such faith in his own ideas. From this point on, he began to fear that the results of the Convention would fall far short of the reforms required. During the two remaining months of debate, he ceased to play the leading role he had seized at the outset—though the nature of the proceedings themselves shifted in a way that prevented any delegate from dominating discussion. Yet Madison was too seasoned a statesman to sulk in his chair. Disappointed as he was with the votes of July 16–21, he now threw his suppport behind proposals that would best accommodate the constitution to his own notions of how government should operate.

The most difficult questions the Convention faced after mid-July involved the executive branch. Madison had given little thought to this subject prior to the Convention—certainly less than had Wilson, Hamilton, and Gouverneur Morris. He was not even sure whether the executive power should be vested in a single President or a plural council. Nor at first did he have a clear understanding of what executive power itself consisted. Like his colleagues, he knew that Americans would reject anything that smacked too much of monarchy—even the limited monarchy of Great Britain. Of one thing only was Madison sure at the outset: the executive had to be able to defend itself against the improper interference of the legislature. But his proposal for the council of revision assumed that neither the executive nor the judiciary alone would have the political strength to resist the legislature.

But if (after mid-July) neither the Senate nor the rejected council of revision could play the role Madison had plotted for them, where would the security against poor legislation now be found? The answer, he gradually saw, lay in enhancing the power of the presidency and making it politically independent of the legislature. But this in turn raised another problem: who other than congressmen would know enough about potential candidates for the presidency to choose wisely? In theory, Madison thought that a choice by "the people at large" was "the fittest" mode of election. But he feared that the free voters of the northern states would always outnumber those of the South; and with other delegates, he found it hard to imagine how voters in thirteen or more states could ever avoid scattering their ballots among a gaggle of candidates. But if, by default, the choice fell to Congress, the President could not be eligible for reelection, since that would encourage him to conspire with his electors. Here, however, the delegates met a further dilemma: what person of honor would seek an office in which good performance and bad alike merited the same reward of involuntary retirement?

When these issues were first discussed in early June, the delegates had accepted the idea of a unitary executive, elected by Congress for a single term of seven years, and armed with a limited veto over national legislation. But these decisions were only tentative, and when the subject arose again in late July, the character of the executive branch became, as Madison later noted, a source of "tedious and reiterated discussions." Now Madison clearly aligned himself with the supporters of a strong and energetic executive. In a lengthy speech of July 25, he endorsed the popular election of the President or the creation of a popularly chosen electoral college, which would meet once within the states and immediately disband—thereby avoiding the risk that the electors would be corrupted.

On the next day, the Convention completed reviewing the amended version of the Virginia Plan that the committee of the whole had reported fully six weeks earlier. It then turned all the resolutions adopted so far over to a five-member committee of detail, instructed to present a more polished draft of the proposed constitution on August 6. Madison was spared election to this committee. But unlike other delegates who seized the opportunity to escape Philadelphia, he stayed in the city. Quite possibly he continued to confer with Randolph and Wilson, the two committee members with whom he was most closely allied.

The committee delivered its report of twenty-three articles on schedule, and on August 7 the full Convention reassembled to begin the new round of deliberations. The time for grand speeches had passed. Mounting impatience to finish the work and go home steadily drove the delegates toward new efficiency.

Much of the discussion went to defining the power of the national legislature and to clarifying the qualifications of its members. The single most important change the committee proposed concerned the scope of legislative power. It replaced the broad and open-ended wording of the Virginia Plan with a long but specific list of the powers the new congress would exercise, including the authority to levy taxes, regulate foreign and interstate commerce, make war and raise armies, and coin money. Imposing as this list was, it no longer envisioned a government acting in every area where the states were "incompetent."

Nor did it meet Madison's standard for national authority, for on August 18, he proposed vesting ten additional powers in the new congress. Some of these involved issues that had embarrassed Congress in recent years but that the Convention had so far overlooked, such as the right to regulate relations with Indian nations, the control of "unappropriated" western lands, and the creation of a national capital. But other provisions better illustrated the wide range of uses to which Madison hoped national power could be put. In proposing that the new government should be able to grant copyrights, establish a university, and make provision for "the advancement of useful knowledge and discoveries," he acted as a man of the Enlightenment who saw the promotion of wisdom and culture as legitimate responsibilities of government. And in further suggesting that the legislature be allowed "to grant charters of incorporation in cases where the public good may require them, and the authority of a single State may be incompetent," Madison looked forward to a government that would foster economic growth by developing turnpikes and canals to facilitate the movement of people and goods across state lines and into new territories.

By late August, then, Madison recognized that the state governments would retain more power than he originally hoped, and through the election of the Senate, greater influence than he thought prudent. But he still struggled to augment national power wherever he could. He favored giving Congress the power to tax exports, to regulate the state militia, and to alter state procedures for electing national representatives whenever circumstances required it. Rather than allow minority interests to obstruct the national good, he agreed that laws regulating commerce should pass by simple majorities, not the two-thirds margin demanded by his colleague George Mason, who feared that northern merchants would run roughshod over southern planters.

Yet while seeking to strengthen the national legislature, Madison also desired a presidency that could check legislative excess. Not until the first week of September was the final shape of the presidency determined. Madison sat for Virginia on the eleven-member committee that proposed the key changes that gave the executive the authority and independence he now thought it required. The President would be elected by an electoral college that would assemble in the separate states, cast its ballots, and promptly disband—thereby eliminating (so the framers thought) the danger of improper influences from the legislature or anyone else. If the electoral college failed to produce a majority, the decision would fall not to the Senate, as the committee originally proposed, but, the Convention decided after three days of debate, to the House of Representatives, which would vote by states. Equally important, the Convention agreed to transfer from the Senate to the President (acting with senatorial advice and consent) the power to make treaties and to appoint judges and other officials.

The Convention approved the Electoral College on September 6. That evening Madison wrote a letter to Jefferson, briefly outlining the major features of the new government. With the Convention so near to a successful end to its labors, Madison should have been heartened by "the extent" of the changes that it would propose, which he well knew would "surprize" Jefferson. But his own views were decidedly pessimistic. "I hazard an opinion nevertheless that the plan should it be adopted will neither effectually answer its national object nor prevent the local mischiefs which every where excite disgusts against the state governments."

Clearly this first gloomy opinion did not reflect Madison's mature judgment of the merits of the Constitution. Nor did these doubts deter him from entering wholeheartedly into the struggle for ratification. Perhaps his disappointment was a measure of his exhaustion, for the demands of debate and his wearying task of daily note taking had clearly worn Madison down.

Yet if nothing else, his discouragement illustrates the strength of the convictions he had carried to Philadelphia four months earlier. So powerfully committed had he been to his own proposals and to the intellectual discoveries upon which they rested that he could not yet fully bring himself to accept the higher wisdom that regards politics as the art of the possible. Believing that in his understanding of the principles of government he had now surpassed the celebrated writers of ancient and modern times, Madison viewed all the decisions that had so diluted his system not as necessary compromises but as fundamental errors of judgment.

It was not, then, James Madison who was inclined to issue a final appeal for unanimity when the Convention gathered to sign the finished Constitution on Monday, September 17. It fell instead to the two great dignitaries—Franklin and Washington—to urge dissenters not to endanger the ratification of the Constitution by withholding their assent. Franklin did so with his usual wit, asking (in a speech that James Wilson read for him) that those who still objected to the Constitution "doubt a little of [their] own infallibility." Washington did so by endorsing a last-minute appeal to increase the size of the House of Representatives. This was the only occasion on which he so much as ventured an opinion during the Convention, and no one was about to cross the commander-in-chief once he had spoken.

Franklin's appeal and Washington's example did not sway the three dissenters—Randolph, Mason, and Gerry—who opposed the finished Constitution. After the Convention first entrusted its official records to Washington's keeping, the remaining thirty-nine delegates proceeded with the signing. While they did so, Franklin gazed at the rising sun painted on the President's chair and mentioned to those sitting near him that "painters had found it difficult to distinguish in their art a rising from a setting sun." He had often looked at Washington's chair and wondered which sun he saw. "But now at length," the sage concluded, "I have the happiness to know that it is a rising and not a setting sun." Then the Great Convention adjourned.

CHAPTER SEVEN

Vindicating the Constitution

❖
❖

A week after the Convention adjourned, Madison was back in New York and Congress. He would have liked to linger en route in Princeton, where the College planned to award him an honorary degree on September 26. But the Convention had decided to submit the Constitution first to Congress, which would then send it on to the state assemblies, who would in turn call for the election of ratification conventions; and Madison intended to see the first step in this process go off without a hitch. His caution was well taken. In New York, he learned that his colleague Richard Henry Lee planned to ask Congress to amend the Constitution before forwarding it to the states. It took three days of strenuous argument to hammer out a compromise under which Congress would unanimously transmit the Constitution without itself voicing any opinion on the merits of the plan.

Madison never wavered in supporting ratification, but doubts about the Constitution still swirled in his own mind. On October 24 he finally found time to provide Jefferson with the summary of the Convention he had promised earlier. The most striking part of this seventeen-page letter was its detailed defense of Madison's original plan to give Congress a "negative in all cases whatsoever" over state laws—a measure he suspected Jefferson would abhor. Madison still feared that the new government would prove unable either to protect itself against the "encroachments" of the states or to secure individual and minority rights against the unjust laws of the states.

Only four weeks later, the single work for which Madison is best known appeared in the New York *Independent Journal*. The Tenth *Federalist* was Madison's first contribution to the series of essays that Alexander Hamilton and John Jay had launched in late October. (Illness limited Jay to writing only five of the eighty-five essays.) Their immediate concern was to promote the adoption of the Constitution in New York, where it faced strong opposition from the political machine of Governor George Clinton. But from an early point these essays acquired a more profound character as the most reasoned and systematic defense of the Constitution. Their reputation has grown ever since.

Such reverence risks ignoring the difference between private opinions and public arguments. The authors had no reason to alert readers to their own continuing doubts about the Constitution. In *Federalist* 10, for example, Madison explained with brilliant rigor why the *national* government would "cure the mischiefs of faction," but he did not bother to note that those same evils would still plague the states. Elsewhere he turned his own qualms about the Constitution to the ironic purpose of reassuring its critics, as in *Federalist* 45, where he explained why "the state governments will have the advantage of the federal government."

Yet Madison did strive to present many of his deepest political insights, and to describe the "compound republic" the framers had designed with close attention to its intricate and inventive character. Under the pressure of congressional business and newspaper deadlines that rarely allowed "for even a perusal of the pieces by any but the writer . . . and sometimes hardly by the writer himself," Madison wrote some twenty-nine essays between late November and the end of February 1788.

Two great concerns dominated Madison's contributions to *The Federalist*. The first required explaining how a powerful national government would strengthen rather than weaken the liberties to which Americans were strongly attached. The second allowed Madison to explore the character of the new Congress, and thus to consider the problem that he regarded as the chief danger to all republics: the tendency of the legislature to "draw all power into its impetuous vortex."

Madison's greatest achievement was to restate in *Federalist* 10 the arguments he had first worked out in his memorandum on "the vices of the political system." Against the hoary theory that stable republics could exist only in small, homogeneous societies whose citizens possessed exceptional self-*denying* civic virtue, he argued that "the latent causes of faction"—that is, of self-*interested* behavior—"were sown in the nature of man." Since one could remove the causes of faction only by destroying liberty itself, Madison reasoned, the remedy lay in "controlling its effects." This could best be accomplished in an "extensive" rather than a small republic. "Extend the sphere, and you take in a greater variety of parties and interests"; and this diversity in turn would prevent improper coalitions from forming and enduring. Furthermore, the "vicious arts" that enabled local demagogues to gain election to the state assemblies would not work at a higher level of politics. Voters in large districts were far more likely to elect men "whose enlightened views and virtuous sentiments render them superior to local prejudices and to schemes of injustice."

What if elections did not always produce these results? Madison devoted many of his remaining essays to exploring the numerous checks that the Constitution had built into the national government and that the division of authority between it and the states would further reinforce. In *Federalist* 39–46, he stressed how much authority the states still held, while carefully justifying each of the enumerated powers the Constitution delegated to Congress. And in his concluding essays on the House and Senate (52–58, 62, and 63), he took pains to answer the allegation that both houses would be far too insulated from the people to protect their rights and interests.

But it was in the intervening essays on the separation of powers (47–51) that he defended the Constitution most ably.

The point of having three independent branches of government, all agreed, was to prevent that dangerous "accumulation of power" that "may justly be pronounced the very definition of tyranny." Many of the state constitutions declared that the legislative, executive, and judicial powers were to be kept separate, but "parchment barriers" alone could not restrain the legislature. Nor could one rely on "periodical appeals to the people" to protect the Constitution against improper acts of government—especially if the greatest dangers were likely to arise from the people's own representatives in the legislature.

The only effective remedy, Madison concluded in *Federalist* 51, was to give each department the "constitutional means and personal motives to resist encroachments of the others." Dividing Congress into two houses vested with different powers would erect a first line of defense against improper laws. But since "in republican government the legislative authority necessarily predominates," the greater challenge was to enable the two weaker branches to resist its "dangerous encroachments." This concern lay behind his statement that "Ambition must be made to counteract ambition. The interest of the man must be connected with the constitutional rights of the place." A President attached to his office would wield his veto to protect the independence of the executive, while lifetime tenure would enable the judiciary to enforce the laws impartially. And beyond these "auxiliary precautions," Madison concluded, lay two further securities: the division of authority between national and state governments and the existence of an "extended republic" with its "great variety of interests, parties and sects."

Throughout his contributions to *The Federalist*, Madison revealed his impatience with traditional axioms of political thought. "Is it not the glory of the people of America," he asked, that "they have not suffered a blind veneration for antiquity, for customs, or for names, to overrule the suggestions of their own good sense, the knowledge of their own situation, and the lessons of their own experience?" But his defense of the Constitution was essentially pragmatic. It rested on appeals to experience, not authority; on a hard-headed justification of specific constitutional provisions, rather than an uncritical deference to hoary maxims. But the real merits and defects of the Constitution, he also realized, were "such as will not be ascertained until an actual trial shall have pointed them out."

Lucid and reasoned as its arguments were, *The Federalist* by itself had little impact on the struggle for ratification. That was determined far more directly by the intense maneuvering that began as soon as the Constitution was published. New York was the nerve center for much of this activity, and from there Madison monitored the progress of ratification with deep concern.

Approval by nine states was required for the Constitution to take effect. Six ratified by early February 1788, and in only one of these, Massachusetts, were its supporters pressed to overcome an Antifederal majority in debate. But in five of the remaining states (Virginia, North Carolina, New Hampshire, New York, and Rhode Island) the Constitution was in serious danger of defeat.

Madison had left Philadelphia thinking he would not seek a seat in the Virginia convention. But the pleas of his friends and the examples of other framers changed his mind. As soon as he finished his last essay as Publius, he packed for home. After a week in Philadelphia and a visit to General Washington at Mount Vernon, he reached Montpelier on March 23.

The election was the next day. Finding many of his neighbors spouting "the most absurd and groundless prejudices against the Constitution," he felt compelled "to mount, for the first time in my life, the rostrum before a large body of people, and to open into a harangue of some length in the open air and on a very windy day." Whether by force of oratory or of reputation, Madison and another Federalist (the same tavernkeeper, in fact, who had defeated him on a similar occasion in 1777) carried the election for Orange County handily.

In other counties results were mixed. The one hundred sixty-eight delegates who gathered with unusual punctuality in Richmond on June 2 divided into two roughly equal camps, with enough members wavering to give real import to the actual debates.

As in other states, ratification depended on several factors. First and foremost, the Constitution had to be defended on its merits against the impassioned oratory of Patrick Henry and George Mason. But many delegates also had to be convinced that the Constitution would protect state and Southern interests against a potential Northern majority. A third question concerned the revision of the Constitution. Massachusetts had attached a list of proposed amendments to its act of ratification, and many Federalists saw a promise to support some changes as a useful way to draw support from moderate opponents—provided that such amendments did not lead to basic changes in the structure of the new government.

At the request of Mason, the Convention agreed to debate the Constitution clause by clause before taking even a straw vote on its adoption. Madison welcomed this decision. His labors first at Philadelphia and then as Publius left him fully prepared to defend either great principles or minor provisions. But in practice this rule proved hard to follow. Patrick Henry ranged so widely, even wildly, in his speeches that Madison felt drawn to answer him as the occasion demanded. He could not match Henry's fireworks, and a "bilious indisposition" sapped his strength throughout the three weeks of debate. Sometimes he spoke so low that the newspaper reporter in the gallery could not catch his words. But his logic and tactical skill provided a potent contrast to Henry's "vague discourses and mere sports of fancy."

The debates went back and forth with little evidence of any shift in the "extremely nice balance" between the two sides. The Constitution would carry, Madison thought, but by only a handful of votes. On June 23 the convention finished its review of the text. The next day, Henry moved that Virginia should adopt the Constitution conditionally, withholding final approval until the other states had accepted the forty amendments he now proposed. And Henry wanted these amendments framed not by the new Congress, but by a second convention free to revise the entire document.

In his final speech, Madison denounced Henry's plan as a formula for chaos. "Previous amendments are but another name" for "rejection," he argued. For the "great contrariety of opinions" Antifederalists had already expressed among themselves proved that a second convention composed of delegates firmly instructed to redress the particular grievances of their constituents would never reach an agreement.

June 25 was the day of decision. The Convention rejected Henry's plan, 88–80; then, "with due decorum and solemnity," it approved the Constitution 89–79, with the understanding that "recommendatory amendments" would be added to the act of ratification. Enough members of the majority now crossed sides to enable Henry's full list of forty amendments to receive the Convention's endorsement. Then, on June 27, the Convention adjourned.

Virginia was the tenth state to ratify; New Hampshire had done so only days earlier. But the accession of the largest and most populous member of the Union was the more critical because of its impact in New York, whose convention was still sitting. There the Federalists were sharply outnumbered, as Madison knew from his correspondence with Hamilton. On July 26 the future Empire State ratified the Constitution—in part because even Antifederalists wanted to keep the national capital in New York City. Again, as in Virginia, a proposal for "conditional amendments" was rejected. But New York did call upon the other states to agree to the second convention that Madison dreaded.

In New York as in Virginia, Federalists profited from early victories scored elsewhere and from the reluctance of moderate Antifederalists to hold their states out of the Union. Yet as Madison surveyed national politics from his vantage point in Congress, the opponents of the Constitution seemed far from routed. While the idea of a second convention gained little support, the issue of amendments was still very much alive. And this had the further effect of making the coming congressional elections a test of the continuing strength of both parties.

Madison's reservations about amendments ran deeper than his suspicions of the other side's motives. He had long since decided that bills of rights were worth little in themselves. Like other Federalists who were anxious to prove that the new government would exercise only limited powers, he argued that a bill of rights would involve hidden dangers. "Can the general government exercise any power not delegated to it?" he asked the Virginia convention. "If an enumeration be made of our rights, will it not be implied, that every thing omitted, is given to the general government?" If only some rights were explicitly protected, would not all other rights not enumerated be left vulnerable?

Yet Madison was not wholly immune to argument. The most telling were those he received from Jefferson, who had gone so far as to hope that four states would withhold approval of the Constitution until a bill of rights was added to it. "A bill of rights," Jefferson wrote, "is what the people are entitled to against every government on earth, general or particular, and what no just government should refuse or rest on inference."

Madison wrestled with this opinion for the better part of a year before answering Jefferson in a well-thought-out letter of October 17, 1788. Madison had not changed his mind about the merits of the issue. He still believed that the chief danger to private rights would arise not from an arbitrary government but from popular majorities who would use government as "the mere instrument" of their desires—and who would never be deterred by the "parchment barrier" of a bill of rights. Only grudgingly did he now admit that such bills might prove modestly useful as a means of teaching the people to curb "the impulses of interest and passion," or on those rare occasions when "a succession of artful and ambitious rulers" might produce a government intent on "the subversion of liberty."

Not theory but politics finally moved Madison to endorse a bill of rights. The adoption of limited amendments, he realized, would reassure many who had opposed the Constitution in good faith. Even more pressing was the situation in Virginia, where Antifederalists had seized control of the assembly. At its fall session, Federalists were a beleaguered minority, and Henry, "old in parliamentary science," played upon "the prejudice and apprehensions of many members" to reverse his defeats in June. By better than two to one, the assembly endorsed the New York call for a second convention. Then the members turned their attention to the election of federal representatives and senators.

Madison had let his friends know that he hoped to gain a seat in the House of Representatives. A Henry-dominated assembly would never send him to the Senate, and besides, he could more easily avoid "the appearance of a spirit of electioneering, which I despise" in a popular election—where his reputation would speak for itself—than among the legislators. But this optimistic forecast erred on several counts. Federalist legislators felt they had to put Madison up for the Senate to have any chance of preventing their opponents from controlling both seats. (He placed third, but received far more votes than anyone expected.) Second, Madison misjudged the depth of Henry's malice and art. The election bill that Henry framed placed Orange County in a strongly Antifederalist district, where Madison's prospects against his friend James Monroe were far from assured. To gain election, he was warned, he would have to return to Virginia.

Madison had hoped to see congressmen chosen without resort to the petty demands of local politics. But much as he resisted the pleas of his friends, the reality of the struggle left him little choice. After enjoying Christmas with Washington, he spent a cold January campaigning actively for election. He and Monroe did their best to preserve personal friendship amid political rivalry. They appeared jointly in several debates—one on a day so cold it left Madison with a touch of frostbite on his nose. But in winter the number of voters he could contact in a district sprawling through eight counties was limited. Madison relied instead on the influence of local notables to whom he addressed carefully worded letters on the fundamental issues.

In these letters, Madison at last indicated that he would support amendments to the Constitution. The "calumnies" and "repeated falsehoods" spread by "antifederal partizans" had portrayed him as opposing not only any change in the Constitution but even a declaration of religious liberty. The charge was absurd, and Madison was anxious to rebut it. But with his usual intellectual honesty, he took care to restate the case against a second convention: it would be better to have Congress propose the desired amendments. He noted that he still did not share the sense of "serious dangers which have alarmed many respectable citizens," and that he hoped the amendments could be largely confined to matters of personal liberty and not extend, for example, to questions such as the power of taxation. His preferred reason for his change of heart was to "banish the party heats, which have so long, and so injuriously prevailed."

Mixed and qualified as his reasons were, Madison took his pledge as a commitment, and so apparently did the voters. Snow and two days of subzero cold kept the turnout low; but the results of the election gave Madison 1,308 votes to Monroe's 972. Elsewhere in the state, Federalists also did well, taking six of the nine remaining seats. After a fortnight of rest at Montpelier, and another week discussing affairs of state with President-elect Washington, Madison returned to New York.

CHAPTER EIGHT

Launching the Government

The two years of intense political activity that led to the adoption of the Constitution were only a prelude to the tasks that awaited the four-score congressmen who straggled into New York in March 1789. The Constitution was not, after all, an end in itself. Its adoption was meant to enable the nation to pursue all those goals that had eluded it under the Confederation: the restoration of public credit, the improvement of trade with Europe and the West Indies, and the development of the west.

Madison had rested his earlier criticisms of American politics on the inability of both legislators and citizens to recognize a permanent "public good" that stood above parochial interests and opinions. The very ratification of the Constitution suggested that Americans could sometimes act as Madison desired. But the politics of the past two years reminded him that potent interests and passions still swirled through the body politic. The tasks ahead seemed no less difficult than the struggles just completed. Scanning a list of his colleagues in the House of Representatives, he found only "a very scanty proportion who will share in the drudgery of business." He foresaw disagreeable "contentions first between federal and antifederal parties, and then between Northern and Southern parties." In late March, he even predicted that the new government would resemble the state governments he so detested. But as always, Madison was intent on shaping the course of debate and decision in ways that reflected his own analysis of the "public good."

Had Madison followed Jefferson's example and composed an epitaph listing his greatest achievements, he might well have asked to be recalled as author not only of the Constitution of 1787 but also of its first ten amendments, the Bill of Rights. His most notable work in the First Congress was to convince his reluctant colleagues to consider the issue of amendments at all. With the Constitution safely ratified, many Federalists felt they could safely ignore the call for amendments, while Antifederalist congressmen grew indifferent to the entire issue because they knew that the changes they wanted would never be adopted.

Almost alone among his colleagues, Madison regarded the question as a matter of prime importance. Robert Morris, now a senator from Pennsylvania, scoffed that Madison had "got frightened in Virginia 'and wrote a Book'"—a reference to his campaign letters affirming his support for amendments. But honor and politics led Madison to take his pledge seriously. As he told the House of Representatives while presenting his proposals on June 8, "principles of amity and moderation" should impel Congress to reassure all those "respectable" citizens who would feel "more inclined to support the cause of federalism" once the new Constitution explicitly recognized certain essential rights. At the same time, he was "unwilling to see a door opened for the reconsideration of the whole structure of the government" or "of the principles and substance of the powers given."

To confine Congress within these prudent limits, Madison in typical scholarly fashion extracted nineteen potential changes in the Constitution from the more than two hundred amendments that the state ratification conventions had proposed. Two of his proposals—never ratified—concerned congressional salaries and the population ratio of the House; two others were general statements of principles of government. The remaining amendments fell under the general rubric of rights.

Privately little had changed in Madison's thinking about the defects of bills of rights; in early August he even described the proposals pending in Congress as "the nauseous project of amendments." Nor did he shield either his doubts or his political motives from the two audiences to whom he appealed: his fellow congressmen and their constituents among a larger public, who avidly read newspaper accounts of the debates in the House (and who were greatly annoyed that the Senate, like the Continental Congress, chose to meet behind closed doors). His major speech of June 8 faithfully stated the views he had voiced in his letters to Jefferson and in his campaign against Monroe. The central elements of his position were all there: the difficulty of enumerating rights, the greater danger from popular majorities than from acts of government, the risks of relying upon "paper barriers." Answering the objections of Federalists and Antifederalists alike, he explained his reasons for both his original misgivings and his recent change of mind, while making it clear that his motives were political as well as principled.

Yet for all this, Madison welcomed the opportunity to enlarge the scope of the liberties the Constitution would be explicitly committed to protect. Thus his original proposal that "no person . . . shall be compelled to be a witness against himself" was cast in language broader than comparable articles found in the state bills of rights. Or again, his proposal protecting "the rights of the people to be secured . . . from all unreasonable searches and seizures" equalled the most expansive statement of that principle in the Massachusetts and Pennsylvania constitutions. So, too, Madison expressed his prohibitions on the abuse of power with the imperative verb "shall" rather than the weaker "ought."

Two of his other proposals deserve special notice. The first, the forerunner of the Ninth Amendment, originally read: "The exceptions here or elsewhere in the constitution, made in favor of particular rights, shall not be so construed as to diminish the just importance of other rights retained by the people; or as to enlarge the powers delegated by the constitution; but either as actual limitations of such powers, or as inserted merely for greater caution." Here Madison sought to prevent the enumeration of specific rights from relegating to an inferior status those left unmentioned—a concern consistent with both his open-ended notion of rights and his fear that the very attempt to define rights could inadvertently create loopholes that could lead to their violation. As finally adopted, this amendment came to read: "The enumeration in the Constitution, of certain rights, shall not be construed to deny or disparage others retained by the people."

The second proposal of particular interest held that "No state shall violate the equal rights of conscience, or the freedom of the press, or the trial by jury in criminal cases." In Madison's view, this was "the most valuable amendment on the whole list." While his other proposals limited the power of the national government alone, here he sought to add to the prohibitions on state legislative authority (already found in Article VI of the Constitution) further restraints in the three critical areas of religion, speech, and criminal law. In effect, Madison belatedly attempted to revive his original intention of creating a national government capable of protecting private rights *within* the individual states, consistent with his belief that the greatest threats to liberty would continue to arise there, and not at the national level of government.

On this proposal Madison again met defeat. Not until the adoption of the Fourteenth Amendment in 1868 would the federal government have a firm constitutional basis for acting as the James Madison of 1787–1789 had hoped it would. But after several procedural delays, Congress finally endorsed Madison's remaining provisions for the protection of individual liberty. All of the first ten amendments that became the Bill of Rights appeared, in seminal form, in his speech of June 8. Among the rights that Madison insisted upon recognizing were free exercise of religion; freedom of speech, the press, and assembly; the right to bear arms; and the protection of fundamental civil liberties against the coercive power of government through such devices as restrictions on "unreasonable searches and seizures," and guarantees of the rights of bail, "to a speedy and public trial" with "the assistance of counsel," and to "just compensation" for property appropriated for public use.

Perhaps the most significant proposal Madison offered was the one now known as the establishment clause of the First Amendment, which states that "Congress shall make no law respecting an establishment of religion." The exact meaning of this language has given rise to endless controversy. Does it prohibit Congress from supporting all religion in any way, or simply from attempting to make any one sect an official state religion, while permitting government to support religion on a non-discriminatory basis? Madison's original language—"nor shall any national religion be established"—seems to accord with the narrower second meaning. The House modified this formula several times, finally proposing that "Congress shall make no law establishing religion." But after the Senate in early September narrowed it to a mere prohibition on "laws establishing articles of faith or a mode of worship," Madison led the House delegation to the joint committee that adopted the final version of the establishment clause. There he certainly worked to restore the broader (if more ambiguous) meaning that the clause in its final form retains. But what he and all other congressmen realized was that the establishment clause touched only the national government. The states remained entirely free to decide the forms and extent of the support that particular denominations or all denominations could receive.

Shepherding the amendments through Congress was a momentous achievement, but in the immediate context of 1789, other items on the congressional agenda loomed far more important. Like all other Federalists, Madison was anxious for Congress to enact vital legislation promptly. Abhorring a political vacuum more than most of his colleagues, he came to New York prepared to take the lead in launching Congress on its course. In this he enjoyed the dual advantage of the reputation he had earned through the struggle for the Constitution as well as the personal confidence of President Washington.

As a charismatic symbol of national union, Washington was incomparable. But the burden of his fame and military experience was a stern sense of formality that did not lend itself easily to the give and take of legislative politics. Nor at first did he even have much of a government to command. Volunteers for office there were aplenty: the President, Madison, and every member of Congress were deluged with letters and visits from needy citizens eager to land a position in the government. But the more important decisions involved the men whom Washington would name to his cabinet—and these had to wait for Congress to organize the executive departments and establish sources of revenue.

Here Madison took the lead by introducing a revenue bill on April 8, 1789—two days after both houses finally mustered a quorum. His plan had two basic features. One set of duties (imposts) would be placed on specific goods imported from abroad, and a second on the carrying capacities (or tonnage) of merchant ships, with American vessels paying the lowest rates, and ships from nations that had entered into commercial treaties with the United States paying less than ships from those that had not. Both schemes harked back to measures Madison had favored for some years: the imposts to the abortive revenue plan of 1783, the tonnage duties to his conviction that only economic retaliation could induce Britain to open its markets in the West Indies and the home islands to American merchants. While the Senate eventually gutted the discriminatory element of the tonnage bill, Madison's imposts were largely preserved in the revenue act that Congress approved in June, too late to cover the annual influx of spring shipping, but in good enough time to give the national government its first income in years.

As soon as the House completed action on the impost, Madison introduced a motion to establish departments of foreign affairs, treasury, and war. This motion quickly led to the first great constitutional debate in the new government's history.

The issue was the President's power to remove subordinate officials. If the Constitution required the Senate to consent to the appointment of major officers, some congressmen argued, did it not follow that department heads could be removed only with its assent as well? Madison strongly disagreed. To divide the removal power between these two branches, he countered, would "abolish at once the great principle of unity and responsibility in the executive department." It was safer to hold the President responsible for the proper administration of government than to risk the confusion of subjecting department heads to two masters. Without such authority, Madison feared, the executive power that Article II of the Constitution vested in the President would be rendered ineffective: a chief executive who could not control his subordinates could hardly "take care that the laws be faithfully executed." By the time the House approved the bill establishing a department of foreign affairs (soon renamed the Department of State), Madison and most congressmen agreed that this authority was inherent in the constitutional grant of executive power.

Madison rightly argued that Congress could never resolve this issue "so calmly as at this time, when no important officer" had yet been appointed whose own character and reputation would "influence their judgments." The insight was doubtless shared by the man who was expected to head the Department of the Treasury, Alexander Hamilton. In *Federalist* 77, Hamilton had noted that the President and Senate would exercise the removal power jointly. But when one congressman cited this passage in the debate, he was quickly informed that Publius "*had changed his opinion!*" Of all the founders of the American republic, Hamilton held the most expansive ideas of executive power, and the most sophisticated understanding of public finance. Bitter experience had taught Washington what happened when governments could not raise money, but not how to raise it. Hamilton had spent idle moments during the war studying the history of banking. His obvious expertise commanded universal respect: Madison regarded him as the "best qualified" candidate to head the treasury. And to the advantage this knowledge provided, Hamilton added the personal confidence that he had earned as Washington's wartime aide-de-camp.

Washington submitted Hamilton's nomination to the Senate in early September. Joining him in the cabinet was Secretary of War Henry Knox, the portly Boston bookseller who had commanded the American artillery during the war. To head the Department of State, Washington nominated and the Senate quickly confirmed Thomas Jefferson. Here there was one rub: the candidate knew nothing of his appointment. Jefferson was on his way home from France, where he had been watching the opening stages of the upheaval that became the French Revolution. Madison knew that Jefferson planned to return to France after a brief visit, but he also thought that his personal desires should give way to the interests of both the republic and their native region. After Congress adjourned in late September, Madison—expecting Jefferson to land at New York—left behind a note imploring him "not to yield hastily to objections. The President is anxious for your acceptance of the trust. The Southern and Western Country have it particularly at heart." Not only would Jefferson bring a regional balance to the cabinet; he could also defend southern interests in the settlement of the west, threatened both by Spain's closure of the Mississippi to American navigation and by mounting unrest among the native tribes of the Ohio Valley.

Protecting the interests of Virginia and the South was much on Madison's mind for other reasons. Near the close of its first session, Congress took up the thorny issue of fixing a permanent location for a national capital—a question that had repeatedly divided the Continental Congress. Like Washington, Madison hoped to see the capital built on the Potomac, where its development into a vital economic link with the interior would clearly benefit Virginia. But other states and cities had their pretensions, and only an extraordinary exertion of Madison's parliamentary skills had prevented a coalition of northern states from passing a bill to place the capital somewhere along the Susquehanna. Madison was so vexed that he was even led to suggest that Virginia would never have ratified the Constitution had it foreseen the sharp maneuvers of its northern rivals.

After Congress adjourned in late September, Madison waited vainly for Jefferson to appear in New York, then set off for Philadelphia. Detained by illness, he finally reached Montpelier on November 2, to find a letter from Hamilton. "May I ask of your friendship," the secretary inquired, to offer his thoughts on additional sources of revenue, "and also as to any modifications of the public debt which could be made consistent with good faith, the interest of the Public and of its Creditors?"

Hamilton's profession of "friendship" was not insincere. The two men had collaborated before—in Congress in 1783, at the Annapolis Convention of 1786 and the Federal Convention of 1787, and in writing *The Federalist*—and Hamilton certainly hoped that Madison would support the financial plans that the House of Representatives had just asked him to draft. But privately he had doubts. In a secret conversation with George Beckwith, the British minister to the United States, Hamilton described Madison as "a clever man" who was "uncorrupted and incorruptible," but also "very little acquainted with the world." Hamilton and Beckwith were both disturbed over Madison's efforts to subject British shipping and goods to discriminatory duties. Where Madison believed that American interests would best be served by liberating the nation from British commercial dominance, Hamilton regarded the promotion of Anglo-American commerce as vital to the economic development of the United States and to his own plans to fund the public debt inherited from the Revolutionary War. Hamilton let Beckwith know that *he* would never support any policy that smacked of "commercial warfare" with Britain.

Hamilton's early apprehensions about the soundness of Madison's ideas were confirmed once Congress reconvened in January 1790. By the time Madison took his seat on January 21, Hamilton had already presented the first of his landmark reports on public credit. As Hamilton saw it, the establishment of public credit required the adoption of a comprehensive plan to fund the entire public debt. He wanted the national government not only to meet its obligations to its own foreign and domestic creditors, but also to assume the further burden of paying the substantial debts that the states had individually contracted during the war. The adoption of this program would, he hoped, secure two vital goals. First, it would create a stable environment within which merchants, artisans, land developers, productive farmers, and European investors could all contribute to the growth of the American economy. Second, encouraging important interest groups to look to the Union to satisfy their claims would give the new government potent political influence to counter the state loyalties that Hamilton (and Madison) had denounced so strongly at the Philadelphia Convention. Well aware that Americans were never fond of paying taxes, Hamilton understood that such support would help persuade Congress to raise the revenues his program—and his deeper vision of American greatness—required.

It took Madison some time to digest these proposals, but by early February he was ready to state the first grounds of his opposition to the emerging Hamiltonian system. Two parts of the report struck him as objectionable. A national *assumption* of state debts would reward states that had failed to meet their obligations to wartime creditors while penalizing those that had. Similarly unjust was Hamilton's intention to fund the entire domestic debt at its face value. Through the long years of national bankruptcy, many of these securities—notes promising payment to Continental soldiers, loan certificates subscribed by patriotic citizens—had been purchased by speculators at a fraction of their original value. Madison accordingly called for a plan of *discrimination* that would give original holders full value but pay speculators less.

Madison's dissent both disturbed and puzzled Hamilton and his supporters in Congress, and they searched for reasons to explain it. One popular explanation was political. Virginians believed—wrongly, it turned out—that their state had paid off most of its internal debt; and they also feared that out-of-state speculators beating the countryside had snatched up much of the national debt remaining in private hands. Madison's constituents thus saw little to gain from Hamilton's plans for assumption and funding at face value—and their vocal outcry was clearly heard in New York. Moreover, by 1790 the state assembly was controlled by former Antifederalists who adopted a resolution denouncing assumption as grossly unconstitutional. Throughout his career, Madison never set himself at odds with his Virginia constituents when their wishes were known. Always sensitive to public opinion back home, he felt compelled to oppose those parts of Hamilton's program that most enraged his countrymen.

Madison's plan to distinguish original and current holders of the national debt had a nice rhetorical appeal—soldiers and patriotic lenders could always be portrayed as more deserving than greedy speculators—but that was its only advantage. The measure was quickly and resoundingly rejected in the House. But his campaign against assumption fared better. Madison whittled away at Hamilton's scheme with an endless series of amendments, until finally the House voted, 31–29, to remove assumption from the larger funding plan of which it was part. But assumption was restored in the Senate, where Hamilton's influence was dominant.

These maneuvers led to one of the most famous bargains in American history. In exchange for relaxing their opposition to assumption, the Virginians would receive support for their bid to build the permanent national capital along the Potomac—with Philadelphia serving as the seat of government in the meantime. The chief piece of evidence supporting this deal is found in a memoir left by Jefferson, who to Madison's delight had finally accepted appointment as secretary of state. As Jefferson told the story, he met Hamilton, looking "dejected beyond description," outside Washington's office one day in mid-June. Unburdening himself to his colleague in the cabinet, Hamilton blamed his dejection on the deadlock over assumption and then asked Jefferson if he would intervene with friendly members of Congress. Jefferson invited Hamilton to join Madison and him for dinner the next evening. There the bargain was made, with Jefferson acting as a mediator. Madison would have to maintain his own opposition to assumption: it would simply be too embarrassing for him to reverse course in a matter that the newspapers had covered so closely. But enough votes would switch sides to enable the assumption measure, amended to meet some of Virginia's objections, to pass with the rest of the funding program.

Jefferson's account oversimplified a more tangled story. But the Compromise of 1790 did involve issues that could be resolved precisely because each side thought it could calculate its specific gains and losses and also because great political principles did not yet seem to be at stake. For Madison, the crucial concern was the aroused feelings of Virginians, and his fidelity to their desires reveals much about his understanding of the new national politics. When he had first imagined how Congress would conduct its business under the Constitution, he had fashioned an ideal of independent legislators debating the true public good in a sober, impartial manner. But the reality of 1790 defied the optimistic expectations of 1787. Congress could not be insulated from a public opinion which—thanks to newspaper coverage of the debates in the House of Representatives—was proving surprisingly responsive to what it read. Virginians were as fascinated as anyone else, but in some ways they were more fearful about the uses to which the national government would put its power. Madison's planter constituents, who lived in a chronic state of debt, mistrusted any scheme they deemed threatening to their immediate welfare. Virginians had to be persuaded that the national government would accommodate their interests as well as those of northern merchants. Modifying the assumption scheme to make it more attractive to Virginia and bringing the national capital and its supposed economic benefits to the Potomac were both means to that end.

For Madison, then, the Compromise of 1790 was a hopeful sign that Congress could find reasonable ways to balance divergent state and sectional interests. His optimism, though, was short-lived. When Hamilton presented his second Report on Public Credit in December 1790, its controversial proposal for a national bank raised constitutional questions that Congress had not faced before. Manageable differences over policy began to develop into more volatile disagreements over principle. Increasingly Madison found himself acting not as the leading mover of the legislation Congress was asked to adopt, but rather as the principal opponent of an executive branch in which he feared his own influence, and even that of Secretary of State Jefferson, was waning.

CHAPTER NINE

Into Opposition

Preparations for elections to the Second Congress went forward in the states even as the maneuvering over the funding bill entered its final stages. With his reputation as a staunch defender of Virginia interests secure, Madison had nothing to fear. Though Congress adjourned in time for him to reach his district before the September polling, he let it be known that reasons of health led him to avoid "a long & rapid journey at this critical season of the year." He presumed "that the circumstance of my being present or absent will weigh little with my constituents in deciding whether they will again confide their interests to my representation." Only his family knew that he had stayed in New York to have "the pleasure of Mr. Jefferson's company quite to Orange," a gentle ride from Monticello. About the time they arrived at Philadelphia, the voters were assembling to give Madison an easy victory.

Throughout their fortnight's ride, the two men competed to pay the larger share of their expenses. Evidently Madison came out the winner, but Jefferson found a way to even the balance after they rode back north together in November 1790. When the horse that Madison had sold him for the trip died shortly after they reached Philadelphia—the temporary capital until the new federal city could be erected on the Potomac—Jefferson insisted on paying full value for his purchase. Madison protested that "a common friend should hear and decide the case," but Jefferson held firm. All Madison could do was refund the excess that resulted from the secretary of state's bad arithmetic.

If only other disputes could be settled so easily! At the final session of the First Congress and during the months that passed before the Second Congress assembled in October 1791,* the fissures within the government continued to widen. Madison became the leader of a "republican interest" opposed to the financial and economic program that Hamilton had launched with his plan for funding the debt. In the cabinet, Jefferson and Hamilton advocated sharply divergent ideas of the nation's foreign policy, especially in their assessments of the implications of the revolutionary upheaval in France and the general European war it provoked. By the time the Second Congress adjourned in March 1793, it was evident that a government established, in Madison's words, to "cure the mischiefs of faction," was divided between two parties espousing different programs and principles and competing at both national and state levels of politics.

The rapid development of this first political party system required creative adjustments in both the theory and practice of republican politics. Madison played a crucial role on both counts. In the process he revised many of the beliefs he had held as the radical nationalist of the late 1780s. For while Madison valued intellectual consistency, he was never a rigid ideologue. He took his lessons from experience, and then converted them into both practical applications and theoretical insights. Both were needed when Hamiltonianism challenged many of his earlier predictions about the likely course of national politics.

Madison and Jefferson had little in the way of either experience or precedent to draw upon when they first moved into opposition. True, the idea that *legislators* often divided into well-defined factions over particular issues was not new. And in a few states—notably Pennsylvania—durable coalitions of *voters* had come to support one party or another in a continuing strug-

---

*Through the nineteenth century, a full year passed between the election of a new Congress and its first session.

gle to control the state government. But the idea that political parties should play a regular role in governance bordered on heresy. It was not easy to distinguish opposition to the policies a government pursued from opposition to government itself. And when issues of war and peace came to the fore—as they did after 1793—opposition to government verged on treason.

In 1787 Madison had accepted the existence of political factions as a necessary evil of a free government. One could eliminate faction, he had noted in *Federalist* 10, only "by destroying the liberty which is essential to its existence," or else "by giving to every citizen the same opinions, the same passions, and the same interests." But the notion that organized parties could actually aid legislators and voters to choose between clearly defined programs was more than he originally imagined. Yet that was exactly the position to which disillusion with Hamilton and his policies drove Madison and Jefferson.

Hamilton and his friends, however, found Madison's movement into opposition equally disconcerting—and puzzling. For his own part, Hamilton professed to treat Madison's conversion as an act of betrayal. Had he not expected Madison's "firm support . . . in the *general course* of my administration," he claimed in May 1792, he would have refused his appointment. On a few issues, Hamilton conceded that Madison's opposition was principled. This was notably the case in foreign policy—though here he waspishly faulted Madison and Jefferson for *"a womanish attachment to France and a womanish resentment against Great Britain."* But Hamilton found other explanations for Madison's enmity for his domestic program more persuasive: the insidious influence of Jefferson (whom Hamilton despised even more); "the expectation of popularity" in Virginia; and the "personal mortification" that both Virginians felt as Hamilton time and again "prevailed" in Congress. "This current of success on one side and defeat on the other have rendered the opposition furious," he concluded, "and have produced a disposition to subvert their competitors even at the expense of the government."

Nothing that Madison wrote during this period, however, suggests that either a personal animus against Hamilton or a pliant desire to please his Virginia constituents drove him into opposition. The latter consideration had affected his position on assumption, but by 1791 Madison's qualms about the Hamiltonian program ran far ahead of public opinion in Virginia. Nor did his change of politics betray a jealous fear that Hamilton had gained the sole confidence of the President. Well into 1793, Washington regarded Madison and Jefferson as trusted advisers. And arguably Madison would have enjoyed greater influence in the House had he chosen to act as chief spokesman for "administration."

The suspicions that brought Madison and Jefferson to oppose Hamilton, then, resulted from their substantive disagreements over policies and principles. A series of developments in 1791 widened the dispute to a point where a reconciliation of these three great leaders became inconceivable.

The first and most critical rested on Hamilton's efforts to consolidate his financial and economic program. For Madison its most controversial element was the national bank that Hamilton asked Congress to incorporate in December 1790. He was less troubled by the additional revenues in the form of an excise tax on spirits that Hamilton secured from Congress in March 1791. Given popular aversion to other forms of taxation, Madison could "see nothing else that can be done." Also alarming was the Report on Manufactures that Hamilton delivered later that year.

Perhaps Madison would have viewed these proposals with less concern had he not been disgusted by the fevered speculation in public securities and bank notes that he observed in Philadelphia while Congress was in session and then in New York after he and Jefferson completed a leisurely swing up the Hudson and down the Connecticut rivers in the spring of 1791. So many opportunities had been opened for speculators to draw corrupt profits, he wrote Jefferson, that "my imagination will not attempt to set bounds to the daring depravity of the times." Well-founded reports that Hamilton's supporters in Congress were also speculating in securities offended him further. As he told Benjamin Rush one evening in 1792, "he could at all times discover a sympathy between the speeches and the pockets of all those members of Congress who held certificates"—that is, government securities.

Part of Madison's opposition to the Hamiltonian system rested on the belief that its benefits would hardly be evenly distributed across the country. The chief beneficiaries of the bank, he suspected, would be the same northern merchants who were so eager to speculate in the funded debt.

But calculations of regional interest explain only part of the intense suspicion with which Madison and Jefferson viewed all of Hamilton's actions after 1791. Hamilton's principles seemed as doubtful as his policies. Now the admiration Hamilton had voiced for the British constitution at the Philadelphia Convention took on a more ominous meaning. As Madison and Jefferson saw it, the plans for a funded debt and a national bank were designed to fasten on the United States the same system of public finance that had enabled a train of British prime ministers to convert a once independent Parliament into a docile creature of their own interests and ambitions. That was why Madison found his fellow congressmen's financial speculations so disturbing. This was the corrupt regime that Americans had rejected in 1776. And the constitutions of government they had written then—and rewritten in 1787—were consciously framed to prevent the vices of Britain from infecting the virtuous republicans of the New World.

This concern with the political implications of the Hamiltonian system best explains why Madison cast his opposition to the bank in the language of constitutional principle. The central issue, he told the House on February 2, 1791, was whether the Constitution had vested a power of incorporation in Congress. Such a power, he recalled, "had been proposed in the general convention and rejected." But that piece of historical evidence mattered less than the broader view of the Constitution that Madison now put forward.

Supporters of the bank relied on a liberal reading of the clause that authorized Congress to "pass all laws necessary and proper to carry into execution" its other delegated powers. In Madison's view, this manipulation of the open-ended language of the Constitution would destroy "the essential characteristic of the government" by giving Congress "an unlimited power" of legislation. Madison insisted that Congress could act only in areas where the Constitution clearly and explicitly authorized it to do so—and the power to grant corporate charters, he held, was "an independent and substantive prerogative" that could not be created by a "doctrine of implication."

This effort to raise a constitutional barrier proved unpersuasive: on February 8, only a third of the House voted with Madison against the bank. But his arguments had a larger significance. By raising the quarrel with Hamilton from the level of policy to the higher ground of constitutional principle, Madison clearly indicated that he had no interest in seeking an accommodation with Hamilton.

Many congressmen could not reconcile Madison's restrictive reading of the Constitution with his reputation as an advocate for a vigorous national government. But in one critical sense, his narrow view of the enumerated powers of Congress reflected his longstanding concern with the ability of legislative bodies to ignore the formal limits on their power. Ironically, Hamilton's broad reading of the "necessary and proper" threatened to confirm just how right Madison had been in 1787 to worry about the difficulty of confining legislative power. Should the Hamiltonian gloss on this clause prevail, Madison feared, the legislative power of Congress could never be effectively limited.

This perception naturally led Madison to emphasize the specific enumeration of the legislative powers of Congress in Article I of the Constitution, but it also prompted him to propose a further rule for interpreting the meaning of the Constitution. The Constitution, Madison suggested, was to be interpreted as it had been understood at the time of its adoption—and in 1788, he argued, both "its friends and its foes" had favored his own limited view of congressional powers. The implication was that the Constitution would never have been ratified otherwise. Nor did Madison think that Congress could ignore its duty to weigh the merits of individual acts of legislation against the higher standard of the Constitution. In

1788 he had reluctantly recognized that the judiciary would finally decide whether a particular law was constitutional, if only because they would be the last to act. But the other branches, he believed, had an equal obligation to support the Constitution.

Having failed to persuade Congress, Madison and Jefferson hoped the President would see fit to veto the bank charter. No constitutional thinker himself, Washington was genuinely troubled by the conflicting claims the debate had raised, and he asked Jefferson and Attorney General Edmund Randolph to brief the dispute. When both supported Madison, he turned to Hamilton for an opposing view. In the meantime, he discussed the issue in person with Madison, and even asked him to draft a veto message—a request Madison happily obliged. But in the end, Hamilton had the last word. On February 25, Washington signed the bank bill.

That action did not persuade Madison that Hamilton's mode of "loose construction" was correct. Much of his opposition to the secretary's subsequent report encouraging national bounties to support manufacturing rested on the same constitutional objection to the misuse of the "necessary and proper" clause. Far from opposing domestic manufacturing on economic or social grounds, Madison and Jefferson both recognized that its growth would contribute substantially to their overriding goal of making the United States economically independent of Britain. One of their concerns about the Hamilton financial system was that it diverted surplus capital from useful investment in manufacturing to the bauble of speculation. But the beneficial results that the support of manufacturing might produce were not to be purchased by further subverting a basic constitutional principle.

The contrasting views that Jefferson and Hamilton offered in their opinions on the bank illustrated the second development of 1791 that widened the breach within the government beyond repair. The executive branch was divided against itself as its two leading heads of departments mounted a bitter struggle over the direction of the government. Just as Jefferson abetted opposition to the treasury program, so Hamilton felt that foreign affairs were too important to be left to the secretary of state. In fact, Hamilton was conducting a foreign policy of his own. Dedicated as he was to maintaining amicable relations with Britain, he held secret conversations with British officials in which he made it plain who was their real friend in the American cabinet.

Washington valued the counsel of both men—and Madison's as well. The President had handled unruly subordinates before, and as a former commander-in-chief used to issuing orders, he may have thought that he could allow his advisers to disagree while still maintaining control of his government. But that hope ran afoul of the third event that quickened the movement toward open partisanship: the decision that Madison and Jefferson took in the spring of 1791 to bring their views directly before the public.

With that in mind, Madison asked the poet Philip Freneau, an old college friend, to come to Philadelphia and begin publication of a newspaper that would speak for "the republican interest" and counter the strong support Hamilton enjoyed in John Fenno's *Gazette of the United States.* After some discussion, they agreed that Freneau would be employed as a translator at the Department of State. That would leave him plenty of time to edit the new *National Gazette*, which first appeared on October 31.

Its publication amounted to a declaration of political war on Hamilton, who soon concluded that the *National Gazette* was "devoted to the subversion of me and the measures in which I have an Agency." Nor did he for a moment doubt who was to blame for the attacks that filled Freneau's columns. By spring 1792, he had decided—though he needed little persuading— *"That Mr. Madison cooperating with Mr. Jefferson is at the head of a faction decidedly hostile to me and my administration."* Soon his own squibs attacking Jefferson as Freneau's patron were being printed (pseudonymously) in the papers; and Madison and Jefferson had little trouble identifying their author.

The fact that this escalating newspaper war alerted the public to the divisions within the cabinet mattered far less than the political calculations upon which both sides—but especially the

Republicans—acted. Finding themselves well short of a majority in either house of Congress, and unable to convert the President to their point of view, Madison and Jefferson realized that an appeal to the public was their only recourse. They hoped, perhaps naively, that aroused public opinion might influence the deliberations of the government. But they also sought to lay the groundwork for making the congressional elections of 1792 a test of the strength of the contending factions.

This was a far more radical step for Madison to take than it was for Jefferson. Where Jefferson had treated even Shays' Rebellion as proof that the American people were still healthily attached to their liberties, the Madison of the 1780s had fretted about the dangers of too much democracy. In 1787 Madison had sought to insulate national politics from a public opinion that he feared was always more likely to reflect private interests and passions than a sober assessment of the public good. Elections, he then thought, were meant not to measure the preferences of voters but rather to identify the wisest and most public-spirited representatives. And in *The Federalist*, he had portrayed public opinion as a volatile threat to the stability of any republic. No one recalled *that* Madison better than Hamilton, who was now convinced that his former ally was becoming exactly the kind of demagogue that both men had denounced only a few years ago.

Madison's changed attitude toward public opinion may have been politically calculated—as Hamilton and his supporters in Congress suspected—but it was not cynical. The simple fact was that the emerging realities of national politics did not conform to his optimistic predictions of 1787 and 1788. With his pragmatic bent toward taking his lessons from experience, Madison adjusted his thinking accordingly. And no lesson was more difficult but also more important to accept than the one that the progress of the Hamiltonian program provided. For the Federalist successes in Congress—catering as Madison thought they did to northern commercial interests—offered a classic example of how an unchecked "factious majority" could equate the particular interests it represented with the broader public good Madison once hoped the national government would serve.

One part of Madison's reaction to these developments can be traced in a series of short essays that he contributed to the *National Gazette* between November 1791 and December 1792. Set next to his earlier writings as Publius, these articles appear half-formed and terse; yet they also suggest the principles upon which the Republican party would appeal for public support.

Madison used several of his essays to hint at the differing economic ideas of the two parties, often echoing the impassioned celebration of rural life in Jefferson's *Notes on the State of Virginia*. Thus in discussing the "Republican Distribution of Citizens," he praised the social and political benefits of agricultural life while disparaging the stultifying living conditions of sailors and artisans—occupations that Hamiltonian schemes of commerce seemed likely to promote. Again, in an essay on "Fashion," Madison found a moral lesson in recent reports of privation among unemployed British buckle- and buttonmakers, whose "servile dependence" on the "caprices of fancy" and trade stood in contrast with "the independent situation and manly sentiments of American citizens, who live on their own soil."

Far more original was the discussion of "Property" that Freneau published on March 27, 1792. In a striking formulation, Madison widened the definition of property to cover not simply the objects one owned but "every thing to which a man may attach a value and have a right"—including civil and religious liberties and "the free use of his faculties." "In a word," he asserted, "as a man is said to have a right to his property, he may be equally said to have a property in his rights." But "a just government," Madison then added, must treat its citizens equally; and that in turn meant that it should avoid measures that granted legal preferences to particular forms of economic activity. The unstated implication was that the Hamiltonian program of bounties and chartered banks was unjust simply because it favored the economic interests of the North.

Essays on topics like these lacked political bite, but other contributions to the *National Gazette* were less shy. In essays on "Consolidation" and the "Government of the United States," he stressed the vital role of the states in "preventing or correcting unconstitutional encroachments" of the national government. The idea itself was not new: he had made the same point in *The Federalist*. But then he had meant only to reassure the fearful, while privately doubting whether the states would ever need to rally their resources against the national government. Now, sensing that the danger was not simply academic, he recognized that his earlier prescription for the balancing role of the states was wiser than he had known at the time.

Through most of his essays, Madison struck a principled tone. Who could deny that Americans should revere all their "constitutional charters," or question the utility of promoting "the mutual confidence and affection of all parts of the Union"? But the continuing newspaper attacks on Jefferson made restraint hard to maintain. In three essays—"The Union: Who Are Its Real Friends?"; "A Candid State of Parties"; and "Who Are the Best Keepers of the People's Liberties?"—Madison portrayed the deepening struggle as a conflict between two groups who differed over fundamental principles. On the one hand, there were the "Antirepublicans" who believed "that government can be carried on only by the pageantry of rank, the influence of money and emoluments, and the terror of military force," and who disdained the constitutional limitations on the government. Opposed to them were those who believed "that mankind are capable of governing themselves"—ordinary citizens who resented special privilege and who, if well informed, would favor a close adherence to the spirit and letter of the American constitutions. These were "the Republican party" who ultimately would embrace "the mass of people in every part of the union."

The idea that a majority of the citizenry would eventually rally to their standard became part of the new Republican creed. But it was not enough to appeal to public opinion alone, either through Madison's high-toned essays or the far more rabidly partisan pieces that Freneau—to the mounting dismay of Madison and Jefferson—was placing in his columns. Other practical steps were needed to check the influence of Hamiltonian principles.

Congress itself remained the first line of defense. As a veteran of many a legislative struggle, Madison was well prepared to exploit his parliamentary skills. In the Second Congress, he commanded a bloc of perhaps eighteen representatives arrayed against a roughly equal number of Hamiltonian loyalists, led by Theodore Sedgwick and Fisher Ames of Massachusetts. But this left half the House open to persuasion on particular issues, and thus spurred efforts to sharpen lines of difference between the factions.

The climax of legislative maneuvers came at the final session of the Second Congress (December 1792–March 1793), when William Branch Giles, a young but militant congressman from Virginia, proposed two sets of resolutions aimed directly at Hamilton. The first of these, calling for a detailed accounting of Hamilton's operations, was approved; but the second, censuring his conduct in the Treasury, was resoundingly rejected. Jefferson probably had a greater hand in preparing the latter than Madison, who thought their introduction was "very unfortunate" because "the session was too near its close for a proper discussion." But this reservation did not prevent Madison from supporting Giles in debate, or from joining the handful of congressmen who voted for each of the resolutions of censure.

By then Madison and Jefferson understood that a change of measures required a change of men. At the elections of 1792 they took their first steps to convert "the republican interest" in Congress into an electoral coalition that would actively seek the allegiance of voters. The whole idea of national political competition was still too novel to make the congressional elections of 1792 a thorough test of the strength of the two factions. Yet party issues did figure prominently in many contests, as both individual candidates and existing political groupings within the states identified themselves as friends or critics of the Hamiltonian program.

Equally revealing was the Republican decision to oppose a second term for Vice President John Adams, who, though no ally of Hamilton's, favored his program. Here Madison, Jefferson, and James Monroe relied on John Beckley, a fellow Virginian and clerk of the House of Representatives, to discuss a suitable candidate with potential allies in New York and Pennsylvania. The choice fell on Governor George Clinton of New York, an old enemy of Hamilton's and a leading Antifederalist in 1788. When the electoral votes were counted, Adams led Clinton 77-50; but the Republicans took heart from Clinton's respectable showing and the degree of interstate cooperation they had mustered.

Party competition would have been even more intense— and cooperation far more necessary—had Washington obeyed his private inclination not to seek a second term. On May 5, 1792, Washington had summoned Madison to his office and informed him that he would prefer "to go to his farm, take his spade in his hand, and work for his bread, than remain in his present situation." Among his numerous reasons, the President alluded to the growing "spirit of party in the government" as well as his own dismay at the well-publicized conflict between his two leading ministers. But if Hamilton and Jefferson agreed on nothing else, they were united in hoping to avoid the political confusion that would occur if Washington retired. Both had argued against it, and Madison now echoed their advice. The best hope for quieting "the spirit of party," he insisted, lay in "the conciliating influence of a temperate and wise administration," something that Washington, who stood naturally above party, could alone provide.

Madison was wrong, but when the time for decision came in the fall of 1792, the President heeded the patriotic (yet also thoroughly political) appeals of his contentious advisers. Had he anticipated the difficulties he would encounter in his second term, much less the personal abuse to which he would be subjected, he would have placed peace of mind above good of country. But that Washington had never learned to do.

CHAPTER TEN

Europe's Strife

❖
❖

Washington renewed his oath of office on March 4, 1793, two days after the Second Congress adjourned. Madison stayed on in Philadelphia another two weeks, and then set off for Montpelier, this time with Senator James Monroe for company. Nine months would pass before the new Congress convened, but as Jefferson soon informed him, events overseas might lead Washington to call it into special session much earlier. For by 1793, questions of foreign policy arising from the general upheaval of the French Revolution were replacing financial and economic issues as the major source of political controversy.

From the moment in 1789 when King Louis XVI summoned the Estates General to its historic rendezvous, the dramatic events in France had commanded enormous interest among Americans. Many Americans saw the changes there—the creation of a popularly elected National Assembly, the radical reduction in the power of the king, the extension of political rights to the mass of the people—as proof that their wartime ally was following their own path toward enlightened free government. As Madison reminded the House of Representatives in 1792, Americans should naturally "favor an event so glorious to mankind and so glorious to this country, because it has grown as it were out of the American revolution." Nor was he stating a radical opinion when he observed, late in 1791, that "The French revolution seems to have succeeded beyond the most sanguine hopes." Indeed, given the low expectations Americans held for a people long subjected to the tyranny of monarchy, aristocracy, and church alike, their progress seemed remarkable.

This benign view survived the outbreak of war between France and the Austrian-Prussian coalition in April 1792—but not the radical turn that French politics then took. In January 1793 the newly proclaimed Republic declared war on Britain and beheaded the king; then it unleashed its reign of terror. Many Americans still thought these developments justified by the strength of the reactionary forces arrayed against the revolution. Americans celebrated French victories; and they greeted as a hero the new French minister, Edmond Genet, when he landed at Charleston in April 1793. But Genet's rash behavior soon proved self-defeating, while his government's resort to terror, its call for universal revolution, and its evident hostility not just to the Catholic church (which many American Protestants found acceptable) but also to Christianity (which they did not) led to growing disillusion with the revolutionary cause.

The outbreak of war in Europe raised fundamental questions of national interest and policy. The United States was still formally allied with France under the Treaty of 1778. Would it therefore have to defend the French West Indies against British attack as the treaty expressly declared? Could Genet commission American privateers to raid British shipping? The United States had good reason to stand by France. Britain still held its forts on the northwestern frontier, and since 1790 it had been aiding the Indian nations of the Ohio Valley in a bloody war against the American army. Support for France might also prove useful in the southwest, where Spain—a member of the reactionary alliance—still blocked American access to the Gulf of Mexico. Yet a policy of neutrality also seemed attractive, especially if Americans could profit from Europe's misfortune by expanding trade with both sides.

On all of these difficult and dangerous questions, the two emerging parties also divided, with Republicans taking the side of France, Federalists that of Britain. But after 1793, the American response to Europe's turmoil involved more than calculations of national interest. The Revolutionary upheaval became one of those great symbolic issues about which ordinary citizens could hold passionate opinions *regardless* of their immediate interests. And as such, it gave the quarrel between the parties the lasting popular impact that disputes over the details of public finance could never have provided.

At home in Virginia, weekly letters from Jefferson kept Madison abreast of the new disputes within the cabinet. The initiative came from Hamilton, who sought to use the change of regime in France to call into question the validity of the treaty of 1778. At his behest, Washington put three major questions to his advisers in mid-April. The first involved determining whether the President should issue a proclamation of neutrality, and if so, what form it should take. The second required deciding whether the treaty of alliance should stand "suspended" until a permanent government clearly existed in France. Closely related to this was a third question: should Genet be received as the official minister of France, or should his reception be somehow "qualified" until the situation in France sorted itself out?

Jefferson favored a policy of "manly neutrality" that would enable the United States to undertake actions useful to France. He also questioned whether the President could unilaterally issue a proclamation of neutrality, since such an act involved issues of war and peace that the Constitution assigned to Congress. For his part, Hamilton suggested that the United States was absolved, at least temporarily, of any obligation to France, and that a policy of impartial conduct toward the belligerents was both appropriate and in the national interest. The President agreed, with Jefferson, that the alliance was not void. But on the key issue, Jefferson did not prevail. Washington issued essentially the proclamation that Hamilton sought and then left his cabinet to work out the details of its implementation. Jefferson found himself a minority of one against Hamilton, Knox, and an "indecisive" Edmund Randolph, whom he regarded as "the poorest cameleon I ever saw." This isolation confirmed Jefferson's intention to resign his post and return to Monticello.

Defeat in the cabinet did not mean, however, that the nation at large would accept the "mere English neutrality" Jefferson and Madison despised. The people so favored France, Madison believed, that "nothing but the habit of implicit respect" would protect even the President "from blame if through the mask of neutrality, a secret Anglomany should betray itself." For this reason, he "anxiously wish[ed]" that a warm reception for Genet would reveal "the real affections of the people" and thus produce a policy more favorable to France. Meanwhile he begged Jefferson to abandon his "longings for the repose of Monticello." But Jefferson, feeling beleaguered "in desperate and eternal contest against a host who are systematically undermining the public liberty," was unwilling to honor this request.

Madison and Jefferson had good reason to think that public opinion was on their side. For one thing, the outcome of the congressional elections seemed to give "the republican interest" a strong boost. But public opinion, as Madison had long known, was fickle, and well before the new Congress assembled, it came under additional pressures.

Most alarming—as the two Virginians saw it—was the conduct of Genet. While his public reception met their most optimistic expectations, the new minister's efforts to exploit his early popularity to the advantage of France were impolitic and ill-calculated. Genet set about commissioning privateers to sail against British merchantmen—and thus played directly into Hamilton's hands by reinforcing the case for strict neutrality. Ignoring Jefferson's repeated pleas, Genet deluded himself that he could appeal beyond the administration to Congress and the people themselves. "Never in my opinion, was so calamitous an appointment made," Jefferson wrote Madison in early July. If Genet's "disrespectful and even indecent" communications with Washington were ever made public, "they will excite universal indignation."

In the same letter, Jefferson pressed a new duty on Madison: to answer the essays of a writer signing himself "Pacificus," whom he correctly identified as Hamilton. In these essays Hamilton not only challenged the validity of the alliance with France, but also raised a central constitutional question by affirming that the President, acting independently of Congress, was well within his powers to issue a proclamation of neutrality.

From this point, Hamilton sought to stake a more potent claim: that the general power to conduct foreign relations was by nature inherently executive, and that Congress could properly act only where the Constitution specifically permitted it to do so. "For god's sake," Jefferson begged, "take up your pen, select the most striking heresies, and cut him to pieces in the face of the public."

When the proclamation first appeared, Madison was most troubled by its implications for the nation's foreign policy. The constitutional issues had not eluded his attention, however, and he soon concluded that the President's unilateral action was constitutionally suspect. But he was not eager to oppose Pacificus. The hottest Virginia summer in memory sapped his energy, and he feared his ignorance of both "material facts" and fine points of international law might lead him into "vulnerable assertions or suppositions which might give occasion to triumphant replies." Nor was he unaware of the difficulty of criticizing a presidential act without also impugning the President himself.

Yet neither could he overlook the consequences of allowing Pacificus to go unrefuted. Hamilton's expansive view of executive power aimed to preempt Republican efforts to use Congress to counter the pro-British policy Hamilton was bent on pursuing. At the same time, Madison hoped to rescue the President from "the snares" Hamilton had set for him. Madison counted himself among Washington's "real friends," and he was genuinely worried that the chief executive's reputation—both political and historical—would be harmed if he naively assumed "prerogatives not clearly found in the Constitution," but which indeed seemed to be "copied from a monarchical model."

The task of answering Pacificus, Madison complained, was "the most grating one I ever experienced." Rather than risk foundering on the details of the treaty or the proclamation, he sought to direct the attention of his readers to the basic constitutional question. Nothing in the Constitution gave the President the discretionary authority Pacificus claimed for him, Madison argued. The power to decide questions of war rested exclusively with Congress; the power to make treaties was shared equally between the President and Senate. Madison did concede that the President could properly prevent American citizens from committing rash acts that could provoke conflict with the warring powers. But the executive had no right to take actions that would prevent Congress from exercising its own powers of decision.

By the time these essays appeared (under the pen name Helvidius) in the *Gazette of the United States* in late August, the situation had moved beyond the point where an appeal to constitutional principle could prove effective. Genet's insulting conduct toward Washington had worked just as Jefferson and Madison feared. Jefferson not only approved the cabinet's decision to request his recall, but also concluded that the Republicans must now accept the proclamation and avoid "little cavils" as to whether the President should have issued it in the first place. Federalists were holding public meetings in support of the President *and* his proclamation throughout the country—even in the Virginia capital at Richmond—and the Republican leaders now felt compelled to prevent Genet's behavior from souring opinion of both France and Genet himself.

The fall of 1793 thus found Madison uncertain what course politics would take when Congress reassembled. In fact, for a while no one could be sure when or where the members would convene. With yellow fever raging in Philadelphia, Washington wrote in mid-October to ask whether he should propose a change in the time and place of meeting. Fortunately, by the time Madison and Monroe set out a month later, the epidemic had ended—though not before hundreds of victims succumbed to the worst outbreak of disease in eighteenth-century America.

It was during the long opening session of the Third Congress that "the Republican interest" in Congress became known as "Mr. Madison's party." On the last day of the year, Jefferson resigned his post and almost immediately set out for Monticello—where he quickly lapsed into political seclusion. His withdrawal left Madison in command of the opposition. Two months passed before he even found time to write Jefferson, who marveled at how little news of national politics reached Virginia. This very lack of information led Jefferson to conclude that "the people are not in a condition either to approve or disapprove of their government, nor consequently to influence it."

Washington would have been happy to have Madison succeed Jefferson at the Department of State. But the thankless role of cabinet dissenter did not appeal to him, and the President turned instead to Edmund Randolph. Madison thought he would be more effective in Congress. With Republicans holding a potential majority in the House, he hoped that Congress would vindicate his constitutional arguments as Helvidius by adopting legislation that would effectively reverse the "Anglo-man" foreign policy that the administration had pursued since the spring.

His major initiative was a set of resolutions that called upon Congress to implement the recommendations that Jefferson had presented in a final report on the nation's foreign commerce. In these resolutions, Madison revived the same plan of commercial discrimination that he had favored for a decade—and failed to persuade Congress to adopt in 1789. The principle of reciprocity, Madison argued, should be the guiding rule of American policy. With Britain still refusing to open its ports to American ships, much less negotiate a treaty of commerce, the time had come to curtail Britain's unlimited access to American markets. Preferences should be given only to those nations—most notably France—that had signed satisfactory commercial treaties with the United States. As Madison saw it, Britain needed American markets to absorb the "superfluities" produced by its manufacturers, while the "true policy" of the United States was to "cultivate the connection and intercourse" with France, which seemed far more willing to purchase the surplus produce of American farmers.

Events at sea led Madison to hope that his policy now stood a better chance of adoption. British efforts to blockade neutral commerce with French ports had already led to the confiscation of American ships, while a British-arranged truce between Portugal and the Algerine states of North Africa allowed Barbary pirates to prey on American shipping in the Atlantic and Mediterranean. Madison predicted that British naval policy would "bring on a crisis with us"—and thus offset the damage done to Franco-American relations by that "madman" Genet.

Events proved Madison right—but not quite with the results he expected. In November 1793, the British government secretly ordered its navy to seize any neutral vessel trading with the French West Indies. The next month, more than 250 unknowing American merchantmen were suddenly confiscated. American merchants, Madison wrote Jefferson on March 12, "have had a terrible slam in the W. Indies." Even Federalists conceded that war with Britain was now possible. Almost immediately, they offered motions to raise an auxiliary army of fifteen thousand men, to lay additional taxes to cover its costs, and to authorize the President to impose a temporary embargo on American commerce. But the key Federalist measure was pacific: to send "an envoy extraordinary" to Britain to resolve the dispute by diplomacy. For this delicate mission Federalist leaders hoped Washington would select Pacificus himself—Alexander Hamilton.

The shock of the ship seizures, Madison agreed, "called for more active medicine." But while he doubted that Britain wanted war, he realized that this turn of events had ironically weakened the case for his "commercial propositions." The proposed mission to London had "the effect of impeding all legislative measures for extorting redress from G. B." At the same time, the military plans of the Federalists seemed expensive enough to "involve this country in the pernicious revenue systems of Europe." The only consolation was "the great mortification" to which Hamilton was exposed when intense opposition to his own nomination as "envoy extraordinary" to Britain led Washington to choose Chief Justice John Jay instead.

The details of revenue and military matters gave Madison and his party much to skirmish over. But when Congress adjourned on June 9, 1794, after its longest session yet, Madison's political hopes of the fall were crushed. Congress was not an easy body to manage. As a result of the first national census, the House had grown from 65 to 105 members, and with fully 60 newcomers in its ranks, a stable legislative majority proved impossible to create with such volatile issues on its table. Even had Madison commanded a disciplined corps in the House, he could not challenge the Federalists' control of the Senate, where by the end of the session the Republican cause lay "completely wrecked."

Finally, and perhaps most important, Madison had to concede that Jay's mission left the initiative over foreign affairs as firmly in executive hands as it had been a year earlier. Madison could not ignore the advantages that fell to the Federalists through their effective domination of the executive branch. "The influence of the Ex[ecutive] on events, the use made of them, and the public confidence in the P[resident] are an overmatch for all the efforts Republicanism can make," he wrote Jefferson in late May 1794. For his part, the President himself still sought to placate both sides. When France demanded the recall of ambassador Gouverneur Morris, a high Federalist, Washington turned to the Republicans for a replacement. After Madison himself declined the position, the President offered it to Monroe, who accepted. But this show of evenhandedness did not obscure his increasing acceptance of Hamilton's ideas of foreign policy.

As this disappointing session of Congress drew to a close, Madison was for once preoccupied with affairs of the most personal kind. In May he asked Aaron Burr to introduce him formally to Dolley Payne Todd. In the conventions of eighteenth-century courtship, this meant that he wished to be considered as a suitor for the hand of the attractive widow who had lost her husband, father-in-law, and an infant son in the yellow fever epidemic of 1793. (Another son, John Payne Todd, survived.) At twenty-six, Dolley Todd was seventeen years younger than the man she at first called "the great little Madison." Born in North Carolina but raised in Virginia, she had grown up in a devout Quaker family. They had moved to Philadelphia in 1783, not long after conscience and the legalization of manumission in Virginia led Dolley's father, John Payne, to sell his slaves.

The bequests she had inherited through her tragic losses of 1793 made Dolley an attractive catch, but Madison's courtship was truly an affair of the heart. He had given no thought to marriage since his brief romance with Kitty Floyd ten years earlier but was now ripe for domesticity. Moreover, the death in 1793 of his younger brother Ambrose and the advancing age of his father, now seventy-one, left Madison far more responsible for the family estate at Montpelier than he had ever been before.

But most important were the many virtues Madison found in Dolley Todd herself. She was vivacious, outgoing, and educated—and it took Madison little time to make his intentions evident. In late May Dolley left town to visit relatives in Virginia, but Madison was not far behind—or far from her in his thoughts. He left Philadelphia a few days after Congress recessed, riding with Monroe to Baltimore (where the new diplomat was to take ship for France), and reached Montpelier by June 24. From this point on, the courtship was conducted by letter—in part because solicitude for a French guest who took ill at Montpelier stranded Madison at home. By early August Dolley had decided in his favor. They exchanged their vows on September 15 at the estate of Dolley's younger sister Lucy, who had married the President's nephew, George Steptoe Washington, a year earlier. The couple spent the next three weeks visiting relations in Virginia, then returned to Philadelphia in mid-October 1794, where they rented a house at 4 North Eighth Street.

Its previous tenant, James Monroe, had arrived in France just as the last spasms of the terror were giving way to the Thermidorean reaction of July 1794—and as the revolutionary armies of France were recording victory after victory on the battlefields of Europe. The turmoil in Paris was fascinating to observe, but it left Monroe, a diplomatic novice, uncertain how to act. Across the English Channel, however, his experienced counterpart John Jay was busy negotiating the treaty that bears his name. Madison was not privy to Jay's dispatches, but he thought that the success of French arms would work to Jay's advantage. "It will be scandalous," he wrote Jefferson early in the new year, "if we do not under present circumstances, get all that we have a right to demand."

Scandalous the Jay Treaty proved to be—though its contents would not be divulged before the Third Congress adjourned.

CHAPTER ELEVEN

Party Leader

In 1794 crucial political developments again took place while Congress was in recess. In the late spring, Hamilton set out to prosecute the large number of backcountry whiskey distillers who had been evading the federal excise tax on spirits ever since its adoption in 1791. His efforts met widespread and sometimes violent resistance, especially in western Pennsylvania, where a clash between protesters and a handful of federal troops protecting the home of Hamilton's chief subordinate produced several fatalities. By late summer, thousands of backcountry farmers joined the protest.

The "Whiskey Rebellion" lacked effective coordination. But Washington thought that these events "were such as to strike at the root of all law and order," and he quickly accepted Hamilton's recommendation that only a convincing show of force would restore federal authority in the backcountry. When the Madisons returned to Philadelphia in mid-October, they found that the President and Hamilton were away in the field, commanding the 13,000-man army of militia they had called into service to crush the "insurgents"—who on closer inspection seemed more like resentful citizens than revolutionary rabble. Madison was disturbed to discover that "the fashionable language" in Philadelphia was that "a standing army" might soon be "necessary *for enforcing the laws.*"

Nor was he pleased when the President used his opening message to Congress to accuse certain "self-created societies" of supporting the Whiskey Rebellion as part of a larger campaign to subvert the government. This was a reference to the Democratic-Republican societies that had criticized the administration's foreign policies since 1793. Since these popular political clubs also supported "the Republican interest" in Congress, the President's crude effort to tar them with the brush of sedition could itself be interpreted as a partisan act.

Madison had no sympathy for the Whiskey Rebellion. He was heartened by the fact that "people every where and of every description" condemned the rebels. But the devious tactics the Federalists were pursuing alarmed him. Insofar as the uprising played into Federalist hands, he wrote Monroe, its "real authors" were "doing the business of despotism." "The game was to connect the democratic societies with the odium of the insurrection—to connect the Republicans in Congress with those societies—[and] to put the President ostensibly at the head of the other party, in opposition to both." Rather than let the game be played that way, Madison prevailed on the House to reply to the President's message with a simple affirmation that "the great body" of the people remained "attached to the luminous and vital principles of our constitution." Madison thought Washington's message "was perhaps the greatest error of his political life." Still viewing the President as the unwary victim of manipulation, Madison misjudged how deeply newspaper assaults on his reputation and policies had hurt Washington. But even so, he knew little would be gained by opposing the President.

The severity of the administration's reaction to the Whiskey Rebellion was ominous, but Madison foresaw that the results of Jay's negotiations would affect national politics more profoundly. Well into February 1795, only odd "scraps" of information about the treaty reached America. Madison struggled to suspend judgment, but privately he suspected "that the bargain is much less in our favour" than either recent French victories or "the justice of our demands" warranted. The "impenetrable secrecy" in which the President kept the treaty when a complete text finally arrived in early March—just after Congress adjourned—confirmed these suspicions. While recalling the Senate to a special session in June, the President refused to release the text of the treaty. Though Madison spoke with Washington on other subjects, on the treaty he remained "as much out of the secret as others."

In April the Madisons returned to Virginia. This was Dolley's first visit to Montpelier, her permanent home for the next four decades. No real news came from Philadelphia until early summer; then a political storm more thunderous than any the nation had yet known broke across the republic. On June 24, the Senate approved the Jay Treaty by the bare two-thirds vote the Constitution required. Defying the majority's ban on publishing the treaty, a Republican senator leaked the text to the press, "from whence it flew," Madison later observed, "with an electric velocity to every part of the Union."

Jay had concluded his negotiations while the troops were still tramping about the rugged Pennsylvania countryside. His instructions had been drafted by Hamilton, whose dominant concern was to preserve peace with Britain. Jay was a faithful Federalist, but rather than trust to chance, Hamilton deprived him of his one credible threat by secretly informing the British minister to America that the United States would not enter a league of armed neutral powers to oppose the British blockade. The treaty that Jay signed in November 1794 was a milestone in several respects, notably in providing for the appointment of bilateral commissions to resolve three outstanding issues: the payment of pre-Revolutionary private debts, British confiscation of American ships, and the boundary lines between New England and Canada. But on the crucial questions of foreign policy, the Jay Treaty seemed to purchase peace through timidity. It failed to gain a single significant concession in the realm of commerce, and it accepted the narrow interpretations of neutral rights that Britain invoked to justify its assaults on American shipping.

Republicans denounced the treaty as a shameful capitulation to Britain, and in popular meetings and newspaper columns, its terms and its American author were pilloried for betraying the very independence of the United States. Madison fully agreed. The terms Jay had accepted, he complained, "would have been scorned by this country at the moment of its greatest embarrassments."

Yet the sources of his opposition to the Jay Treaty ran far deeper. What the treaty finally confirmed, he realized, was that the issues that divided Hamiltonians and Republicans rested on something more profound than their opinions of the French Revolution or the British constitution—important as these were. For Hamilton, the encouragement of Anglo-American commerce was absolutely essential. His entire financial program depended on the continued collection of duties on the imports that Britain alone could provide in quantities adequate to meet the demands of both American consumers and the national treasury. Next to the benefits of preserving the commercial connection with Britain, Hamilton counted the political embarrassment of the Jay Treaty as a marginal cost.

For Madison, by contrast, the requirements of public credit could never justify sacrificing the economic independence of the United States. Regarding Britain as a predatory power, Madison thought that the long-term interests of the United States would be better served by policies that opened up American trade with other nations. All of his thinking about commercial policy rested on this assumption. He objected to the treaty not merely because Jay had struck so poor a bargain, but more important, because the treaty exposed just how closely wedded the Hamiltonians were to financial and commercial policies that Madison thought would thwart the development of an independent American economy.

In August Washington swallowed his own considerable doubts and signed the treaty, thus completing its ratification—and laying himself open to unprecedented criticism in the press. The newspaper war over the treaty continued unabated. Republican criticisms were answered at length—and effectively—by Hamilton, who remained the guiding genius of his party even after leaving the cabinet in January to return to the practice of law. Like Patroclus urging Achilles to stop the rampaging Hector, Jefferson urged Madison to enter the lists against Hamilton one more time. "In truth, when he comes forward, there is nobody but yourself who can meet him." This time Madison balked. He was willing to send detailed criticisms of the treaty to his correspondents. But he had his eye less on the public than on the new Congress that would meet in December 1795.

The Jay Treaty was now the supreme law of the land. But Madison hoped that its massive unpopularity and the growing Republican strength in the House could somehow prevent its implementation and thus undermine the Federalists, who had become "a British party systematically aiming at an exclusive connection with the British government."

Two obstacles stood in his way. Since the Consitution excluded the House from any share in the treaty power, it was not clear how the lower chamber could even consider, much less oppose a duly ratified treaty. The "real obscurity in the constitutional part of the question," Madison understood, would complicate the task of welding all who opposed "the treaty on its merits" into an effective majority. With thirty-nine newcomers in the House, it would take time to test the strength of the parties.

This "truly perplexing" situation demanded caution, Madison thought. The trick was to affirm the right of the House to participate in treaty making without allowing the Federalists to drape their defense of the treaty with the mantle of Washington's prestige. The fact that the establishment of the arbitration commissions required the appropriation of public funds might sustain the claim that the House was entitled to judge the treaty on its merits. So did other articles relating to commerce, since the Constitution vested the power to regulate foreign commerce in Congress (not simply the Senate).

But how, exactly, were these claims to be asserted? When Washington sent the officially ratified copy of the treaty to Congress on March 1, 1796, Madison's concern about the difficulty of molding a reliable coalition of Republican congressmen was immediately confirmed. He voted with the substantial majority to adopt a resolution to ask the President to place Jay's instructions and other documents regarding the negotiations before the House. Washington rejected the call for papers in a stinging message asserting that only an inquiry of impeachment could constitutionally justify such a request. The President's "absolute refusal was as unexpected as the tone and tenor of the message are improper and indelicate," Madison informed Jefferson. In a novel effort to maintain party cohesion, the Republicans in the House held their first caucus to ponder their response. The caucus failed to reach a binding consensus, but it produced enough agreement to enable Madison to take the lead in renewing the call for documents. On April 6, he offered "a free but respectful review of the fallacy" of the President's position. To his surprise, his arguments went unrebutted, and the next day the House reaffirmed its rights by a majority of twenty.

While this vote did not budge the President from his own claim of executive privilege, it cleared the way for debate on the decisive issue of implementing the treaty. Through mid-April, Madison struggled to hold his working majority intact. He knew that "vast exertions are on foot without and within [the] doors" of Congress to shift the balance of votes. Federalist sponsored meetings in major cities and New England were producing petitions urging acceptance of the Jay Treaty. Patriotic appeals to support the President alternated with fevered warnings that repudiating the treaty would lead to war with Britain. Hamilton mobilized the mercantile community to exert all its influence in behalf of the treaty. These had their effect, and so did an impassioned speech by the sickly but brilliant Massachusetts congressman, Fisher Ames. When the crucial votes came on April 29–30, the unexpected absence of two Republicans allowed the Federalists to claim victory by the narrowest margin possible.

After five months of intense political maneuvering, Madison took this defeat all the worse because he traced it more to "the unsteadiness, the follies, the perverseness, and the defections among our friends" than to "the strength, or dexterity, or malice of our opponents." With both an unpopular treaty and an apparent majority in the House to exploit, the Republicans had again been overcome by "the name of the President and the alarm of war," he wrote Jefferson. "A crisis which ought to have been so arranged as to fortify the Republican cause" had instead "left it in a very crippled condition." Meanwhile, private letters from Monroe confirmed his fear that the French interpreted the Jay Treaty as clear evidence that the United States was pursuing a foreign policy favorable to Britain.

Madison's campaign against the Jay Treaty marked the real conclusion of his congressional career. One lesson now stood uppermost in his mind. After five years of futile efforts to make Congress an effective barrier against Hamiltonianism, Madison understood that control of the executive branch was the key to directing national policies. But the Republicans could hope to capture the presidency only if Washington stepped aside.

Madison had thought since February that Washington would indeed retire to Mount Vernon. The Republicans, he told Monroe, were agreed that Jefferson was their only credible candidate against Vice President John Adams, the heir apparent. The fact that Washington held off announcing his retirement until September allayed Madison's fear that Jefferson would disrupt Republican plans by a public declaration of non-candidacy: Jefferson could hardly refuse to run for an office that was not yet available. But Washington's delay also left the party little time to mount a serious effort in behalf of its reluctant champion, the farmer of Monticello.

By all appearances, Madison was no more active than his friend. At home in Virginia, he avoided paying the candidate a visit; and if the two men even wrote each other, they went to the unusual step of destroying their letters. The task of organizing the Republican campaign fell to party managers like John Beckley and Aaron Burr, who worked with great energy and ingenuity to coordinate the selection of right-minded electors in the sixteen states of the Union. They came surprisingly close to succeeding. When the ballots were tallied in Congress, Adams had 71 electoral votes to Jefferson's 68. Support for both men was sectional, but Republicans were encouraged that Jefferson carried populous Pennsylvania, which was emerging as a crucial battleground.

As runner-up, Jefferson became Vice President. He had served with Adams in the Continental Congress and again in the American diplomatic corps—perhaps this "antient friendship" might give him a helpful influence over the second President. But Adams, for all his "integrity," was vain, stubborn, and antirepublican. Expecting few changes in policy, Jefferson suggested that he would act not as a member of the new administration but merely as the presiding officer of the Senate. Madison was no more optimistic. "I cannot prevail on myself to augur much that is consoling from him," he wrote Jefferson in late January 1797.

Two months later, the Madisons were back at Montpelier, learning to enjoy the political retirement that Jefferson dreaded abandoning. Though neither man quite realized it at the time, they were exchanging more than personal situations. Even as a presidential candidate, Jefferson had been only the titular leader of his party. It was Madison, from his post in Congress, who came closest to being the guiding genius of the loose Republican coalition. Now their positions were reversed. However little power Jefferson wielded as Vice President, he was the most conspicuous Republican officeholder around, and as he warmed to the task, he soon became the party's active leader.

Madison, by contrast, was a private citizen at last. Retired from Congress, refusing even to take a seat in the Virginia assembly—much less the governorship of the state, which he could have had for the asking—Madison, at age forty-six, had a new vocation: gentleman farmer. Not since his departure for Princeton in 1769 had he spent a full year in Virginia; now he would not leave his native state until Jefferson's inauguration in 1801 called him back to public office at the new capital of Washington.

Political frustrations and family concerns eased Madison's transition from public leader to private farmer. At age seventy-four, his father could no longer manage the family estate—the largest in Orange County—on his own. As eldest son, Madison was naturally expected to assume the leading role. And with tobacco prices plummeting, active management was needed. Like other planters in the Virginia piedmont, the Madisons were shifting from tobacco to the crops of grain that the combination of population growth and war in Europe made increasingly profitable.

At the same time, Madison set about making Montpelier a more comfortable seat for his own little family—perhaps inspired by Jefferson's endless improvements at Monticello. From the front porch of Montpelier, they had a magnificent view of the Blue Ridge mountains, almost thirty miles to the west. The gently sloping lawn that led up to the house offered a fine playing field for the many nieces and nephews who visited regularly from their homes on nearby farms. Whatever regret the Madisons felt over their inability to produce a child was balanced at least in part by this extended family. And Madison took affectionate and deep interest in raising Dolley's surviving son.

This pursuit of the very happiness to which Jefferson had alluded in the Declaration of Independence was marred only by the knowledge that everything the Madisons enjoyed rested on their ownership of black slaves. At the Constitutional Convention, Madison had denounced slavery based on "the mere distinction of color" as "the most oppressive dominion ever exercised by man over man," while Dolley's Quaker father had so detested the system that he had freed his slaves and taken his family from Virginia to Philadelphia. Madison was not willing to follow that example. Moral abhorrence of slavery led him to act the part of humane master. But in the final judgment, he was no better prepared to live without slaves than the other members of the great planter class to which his family belonged.

For a brief few months, Madison may have hoped his retirement from public life would prove permanent. But his interest in politics never slackened, and the new year of 1798 brought developments that led him back to office.

CHAPTER TWELVE

A Beleaguered Minority

The Jay Treaty quickly brought relations with France to a near crisis. By the fall of 1796, French privateers sailing from the West Indies had begun to capture American merchantmen. In March 1797 the government of the Directory declared American ships carrying British goods subject to confiscation, and it rejected the diplomatic credentials of Charles C. Pinckney, who had been sent to replace James Monroe. When Congress met in special session in May to deal with these developments, President John Adams proposed plans to ready the nation's forces to repel a French invasion. At the same time, Adams sent a commission composed of his old friend Elbridge Gerry, Pinckney, and John Marshall (the future chief justice) to Paris to explore avenues of reconciliation.

Adams had seriously considered sending Madison to France, even going so far as to ask Jefferson whether his friend would accept such an appointment. Including Madison in so crucial a mission might convince both the French and the Republicans of his sincere commitment to peace. (Unknown to Adams, Hamilton also favored sending Madison.) Though still in Philadelphia when this feeler went out, Madison left it to Jefferson to disabuse the President of the idea. Personal wishes alone precluded the mission: in addition to his duties at Montpelier, Madison had a lifelong fear that foreign travel would ruin his health. But even before Jefferson could relay Madison's reply, Adams learned that the cabinet he had inherited from Washington were dead set against sending Madison anywhere but home.

Convincing doubtful Republicans of his good intentions while controlling a Federalist party that looked to Hamilton for leadership was more than Adams could manage. His independence of mind and stubborn self-righteousness did not lend themselves to effective political leadership. And in the rancorous atmosphere of the 1790s, the delicate foreign policy he hoped to pursue—arming for war while negotiating for peace—was liable to be misconstrued in both countries. For as Madison saw it, the Jay Treaty "placed such difficulties in the way of an adjustment" of relations with France "that nothing but the most cordial dispositions on both sides can overcome them." And there was little cordiality in the President's bellicose remarks about France. Madison would not give Adams the benefit of the doubt. By the winter of 1798, he was describing Adams in terms as harsh as any he had ever used against Hamilton or Patrick Henry. "Our hot-headed executive," he complained, was "a perfect Quixote of a statesman," governed by "violent passions and heretical politics."

True, "folly" seemed to rule on both sides of the Atlantic—especially when in April 1798 the country learned of the bizarre reception the American commission had met in Paris. Agents of Talleyrand, the Directory's foreign minister, had demanded that the Americans pay a bribe to gain access to their superior. When the commissioners refused, they were denied official recognition, and their mission went unfulfilled.

Madison was flabbergasted less by the "depravity" of this clumsy solicitation than "its unparalleled stupidity." Even then he was more alarmed by the uses to which the administration could put the affair. The shoddy treatment given the commissioners could be used "for the general purpose of enforcing the war measures of the Executive." Worse, the sensational news from Paris also served the "purpose of diverting the public attention" from "the more important" fact that "the speech and conduct of the President" remained "the great obstacle to accommodation."

Madison's judgment of the President's motives was unduly harsh: Adams was neither warmonger nor demagogue. But Madison was essentially correct in his analysis of the thrust of Federalist measures. With the public aroused over the mistreatment of the commissioners, the Federalist-dominated Congress that met in the spring of 1798 adopted a radical program for building up the armed forces, levying new taxes, and strengthening their party at the expense of their hapless Republican opponents. For as the threat of war grew ever more real, the Federalists enjoyed a powerful pretext for equating Republican criticism of their policies with a traitorous loyalty to the nation's enemy.

The Sedition Act of 1798 was the critical element of the Federalist war program. Its provisions subjected to criminal prosecution anyone who wrote, spoke, or published "any false, scandalous and malicious writing" against any member or branch of the federal government. Federalists argued that the act merely put in statutory form the common law doctrine of seditious libel, which made excessive criticism of the government a potentially criminal act. (Indeed, the Act reformed existing law by allowing defendants to invoke the truth of a statement as a defense against the charge of sedition.) Republicans replied that the Act clearly violated the First Amendment to the Constitution, which barred Congress from making laws "abridging the freedom of speech, or of the press." The Federalists' reliance on English practice marked one more effort to corrupt the free government of the United States with monarchical principles. The Republicans also objected to several other laws Congress adopted in 1798. The most notable, the Alien Act, authorized the President to deport any alien he deemed dangerous to the national security.

The controversy over the Sedition Act forced Americans to consider the meaning of freedom of speech and the press far more carefully than they had while adopting the Bill of Rights only a few years earlier. But the deeper understanding of these principles that emerged *after* 1798 was won at a high cost. For

President Adams and his party regarded the Sedition Act not as a mere deterrent to be used in extreme cases, but as a handy club to beat their critics into submission. The administration prosecuted offenders vigorously, and a judiciary that was Federalist to a man upheld the convictions. And just in case the Sedition Act prove unequal to the task, some Federalists were prepared to go even further. The new provisional army was placed under the nominal command of the retired Washington. But its real leader was Hamilton, his second in command; and the *eminence grise* of the Federalist party was itching for an excuse to march the troops through the Republican strongholds of Virginia.

In reaction to this intense Federalist effort, Jefferson and Madison moved toward more radical positions in the fall of 1798. Time and again since 1793, Madison had ruefully pondered the advantages that the executive branch enjoyed in foreign affairs. "The Constitution supposes, what the history of all government demonstrates, that the executive is the branch of power most interested in war, and most prone to it," he wrote in April 1798. "It has, accordingly, with studied care, vested the question of war" in Congress. But in practice the President could often force Congress to support his unilateral actions. The people were as easily gulled as their representatives. "The management of foreign relations appears to be the most susceptible of abuse of all the trusts committed to a government," Madison observed, "because they can be concealed or disclosed . . . as will best suit particular views; and because the body of the people are less capable of judging, and are more under the influence of prejudices, on that branch of their affairs, than of any other."

But with both Congress and public opinion under the sway of the war fever of 1798, and the administration using the Sedition Act to rein in its critics, where were Republicans to turn? The surprising answer to which Jefferson and Madison were driven was the state legislatures. After conferring at Montpelier in early July and again at Monticello in October, the two men agreed on the general strategy of having the legislatures of Virginia and Kentucky—both controlled by Republicans—denounce the Alien and Sedition Acts as unconstitutional. In the fall, they drafted resolutions—Jefferson for Kentucky, Madison for Virginia—which trusted lieutenants introduced in the two assemblies.

The idea of encouraging state legislatures to take stands on national issues was not radical, given their role in the election of the Senate. What was radical was the stand that Jefferson and Madison asked them to take. Both men agreed in their fundamental view of the Constitution as a compact among the states vesting certain limited powers in a national government. "In case of a dangerous, palpable, and dangerous exercise of other powers not granted by this compact," the states retained some right to protect their own authority and the liberties of their citizens against the abuse of federal power.

But in explaining how this protection would be provided, the two men's positions diverged. Jefferson spoke of the right of a state to "nullify" illegitimate federal acts, implying that it could *legally* prevent the execution of an unconstitutional law. Madison more cautiously declared that the states could "interpose for arresting the progress of the evil." This seemed to suggest that the states should act *politically* to rouse broad opposition to acts of federal usurpation, presumably by approving resolutions that would call either Congress or the people back to their senses and the proper meaning of the Constitution.

That meaning, Madison thought, was to be "limited by the plain sense and intention" of the Constitution as the original "parties" to the "compact" had understood it. But in developing his arguments against the Alien and Sedition Acts, he could not ignore the changes that had taken place in his own thinking since the late 1780s. Then his entire analysis of the vices of the Confederation had presumed that the states would always prefer their own narrow interests to the general good of the Union. He had similarly felt that liberty would face its greatest dangers not from arbitrary acts of government but from the interests of the popular majorities it represented. And bills of rights, he had also concluded, would provide only a weak defense against majorities bent on pursuing their own ends.

Experience had since proved these expectations wrong, and Madison adjusted his thinking accordingly. Whether one regarded the Federalists as an aristocratic clique who had some-how seized power or a factious majority manipulating public opinion, they had clearly breached the defensive lines of the Constitution's scheme of separated powers. With the Federalists dominating every branch of the national government, Madison now understood that the independent existence of the states had advantages he had overlooked in 1787, if only by providing the Republicans safe havens where they could regroup and plan future operations.

Yet Madison did not have to cross uncharted ground to occupy the positions that he took in 1798. In *Federalist* 46, for example, he had surveyed the various ways in which the states could counter efforts by the federal government "to extend its power beyond its due limits." And in his exchanges with Jefferson on the issue of amendments, he had conceded that a bill of rights could provide "good ground for an appeal to the sense of the community" in case "usurped acts of the government" threatened liberty. Privately he had doubted whether either the states or a bill of rights would be needed to resist "encroach-ments" from the national government. But it is a mark of the brilliance of his original analysis of the Constitution that he could revive points he had once made more for purposes of argument than from conviction and apply them to events he had not foreseen.

Madison knew how far he had come since 1789, and he knew the dangerous conclusions to which the positions of 1798 led. That is why, in January 1799, he asked Jefferson to consider whether the Kentucky resolutions did not go too far by implying that a state legislature could nullify any act of Congress that it found objectionable. That was a formula not for opposition but for disunion—and disunion was the absolute evil Madison could never imagine, even though Jefferson, in an inspired moment in August 1799, hinted it might prove necessary. Madison was quick to argue that so gloomy a conclusion was pre-mature, and Jefferson, again accepting his friend's tutoring, drew back.

The true challenge, as Madison saw it, was to recapture the national government from its Federalist masters. Well into 1799, that challenge seemed more than the Republicans could surmount. With American ships sweeping French privateers from the Atlantic coast and the West Indies, war fever remained high throughout the country. John Adams had never been so popular, while Federalist candidates ran well in the elections for the Sixth Congress, even winning eight of Virginia's nineteen seats in the House. Nor did Madison and Jefferson find much to cheer in the reaction that the Virginia and Kentucky resolves evoked from other legislatures. None was willing to endorse the Republican position, much less join a united campaign to repeal the detested legislation.

These developments brought Madison's brief retirement from public office to an end. Accepting election to the autumn 1799 session of the Virginia assembly, Madison, though weakened by dysentery, poured his labors into the preparation of a report justifying the resolutions of 1798. If nothing else, Madison and Jefferson hoped this report would serve as a campaign document for the coming presidential election. But Madison's effort was too detailed and studied to command close attention.

In political terms, another act that the assembly adopted proved far more important. Rather than continue to allow the states' twenty-one presidential electors—the largest bloc in the country—to be chosen by voters in individual districts, a narrow Republican majority approved a new law providing for the election of a statewide slate. This would prevent the Federalists from picking up any electoral votes in Virginia—and in the close race that everyone expected, every vote was sure to count. In most other states, electors were chosen not by the voters but by the state legislatures, making the assembly elections of 1799 and 1800 the crucial battlegrounds.

There was never a doubt that Jefferson would again carry the Republican standard. The reluctant candidate of 1796 had become an active party leader, defining positions, circulating campaign literature, and corresponding with key Republican leaders in the states. The very complexities of the electoral system inspired both parties, despite their inexperience, to be creative in their efforts to attract voters and coordinate activities across state lines. Party organization proved crucial in Pennsylvania and New York, where the race seemed especially competitive. A Republican victory in the New York elections of April 1800 was the first promising sign that the Federalist days were numbered.

But the most important developments shaping the election of 1800 took place within the ruling administration and party. However much Madison doubted the President's motives, John Adams had sought peace, not war. In the fall of 1799, Adams sent a second mission to Paris. Though (as always) a full year passed before its results became known, this initiative infuriated the Hamiltonian wing of his party, and placed Adams at odds with most of his cabinet and with prominent Federalist congressmen. In May 1800 Adams purged the cabinet of his disloyal subordinates, thereby precipitating an open break with Hamilton. For his efforts at restoring peace with France, Adams retained a measure of personal popularity, and he remained the Federalist candidate for re-election. But the turmoil within his party, following hard upon the Republican success in New York, doomed his chances.

Madison's role in the campaign was confined to Virginia. From Montpelier he followed the progress of the election with intense interest and his usual caution. Once the disputes wracking the Federalists became known, he rejoiced to see "the party which has done the mischief . . . so industriously cooperating in its own destruction." But he also feared that the desperate Federalists might try "every stratagem . . . that may afford a chance of prolonging their ascendancy."

One stratagem of which Madison was probably not aware was hatched by Hamilton, who hoped to rig the Federalist electoral votes so that Adams would finish behind his running mate, Charles C. Pinckney. As it turned out, Adams gained 65 votes in the Electoral College, one more than Pinckney. It was the Republicans who failed to insure that *their* vice-presidential candidate, Aaron Burr of New York, would trail Jefferson. Each had 73 votes in the Electoral College, well short of the majority needed to avoid throwing the decision into the House of Representatives, where the Federalists controlled enough votes to bar Jefferson's election. Burr had earlier indicated that he had no desire to supplant Jefferson, but now he refused to say whether he would reject the presidency if the House offered it to him.

At Montpelier, Madison could only fret about the bizarre events unfolding at the new capital of Washington. Burr could not be elected, since that would require defections from Republicans loyal to Jefferson. But ever mistrustful of both the outgoing President and his party, Madison feared that the Federalists might simply prevent any choice from taking place, throwing the nation into a dangerous "interregnum." Though Hamilton urged his allies to accept Jefferson's election, Federalist congressmen wanted to see what course Burr—a man who always had his eye on the main chance—could be induced to take. Only after the House cast 35 fruitless ballots did enough Federalists abstain to allow a vote of ten states to make Thomas Jefferson the third President of the United States.

Madison's relief at this turn of events was tempered by personal sorrow. On February 27, 1801, "rather suddenly, though very gently, the flame of life went out" for James Madison, Sr. His namesake had hoped to join Jefferson shortly after his inauguration on March 4; now the need to settle his father's estate postponed his departure. Madison did not entirely regret the delay. Although he had already agreed to serve as secretary of state, Madison preferred to avoid "appearing on the political theatre" before he had been confirmed for his new office, lest his early arrival confirm the charges of self-seeking ambition that had been directed against him during the rancorous era that the two Virginians now hoped was coming to an end.

CHAPTER THIRTEEN

Secretary of State

Like other Virginia leaders, James Madison hoped that the new federal city of Washington would develop into a major urban center linking Virginia with the interior. When the Madisons arrived there in May 1801, it took vision indeed to imagine a grand city arising from its half-finished buildings scattered amid stands of pine trees on swampy ground along the Potomac River. Many congressmen would rather have been in Philadelphia. Perhaps Madison, in ill health much of the year, also missed the amenities of the northern city. But by the fall the Madisons were able to occupy the three-story brick house built for them two blocks from the presidential mansion—where Dolley and her sister Anna often acted as hostesses for the widower Jefferson.

For all the reverses they had met during their years in opposition, the new President and his secretary of state had felt that the Federalists could not hold power indefinitely. The people would eventually come to their senses. But the Republican leaders regarded the revolution of 1800—as Jefferson called it—more as a vindication of their principles than a victory for their party. Their goal was not to insure continued Republican dominance but rather to bring party conflict itself to an end. The Republican party could not disband immediately; it would need to operate at least until any prospect of a Federalist revival had disappeared. But at that point, Jefferson and Madison hoped, a politics above party would again prove possible. This goal was

133

consistent with the Madisonian ideal of 1787–1788, which had presumed that while the *sources* of partisan behavior would always exist, the proper purpose of republican politics was to define a higher notion of the common interest.

As secretary of state, Madison performed a number of routine tasks relating to domestic affairs, but his major responsibility was the conduct of foreign relations. It was a demanding job because the diplomatic agenda of Jefferson's two terms was filled with subjects of the first importance: the Louisiana Purchase of 1803, ongoing attempts to convince Spain to cede Florida, and efforts to maintain the rights of neutrality against both Britain and France. Jefferson, of course, was fully qualified to serve as his own secretary of state, and it soon became clear that Jefferson was the superior—as the Constitution insisted he must be. Yet it is equally true that no President and secretary of state ever worked together more harmoniously. The two men shared a common view not only of the national interest but also of the world beyond America. In crucial ways, Madison saw that world through the eyes of the Jefferson who had recoiled against the gross inequities of the aristocratic societies he had observed during his diplomatic service in the 1780s.

For once, events overseas favored the Republicans by making questions of foreign policy less urgent than they had been since 1793. The most dramatic developments occurred in France, where the military hero Napoleon Bonaparte had seized power in November 1799. Napoleon bore no affection for the United States, but he and foreign minister Talleyrand wanted to end the hostilities between the two countries. In October 1800, the American peace commissioners signed an acceptable peace agreement in Napoleon's presence. One year later, Britain and France signed an armistice ending the general conflict that had raged since 1792.

Napoleon's accession ended whatever loyalty the Republicans still felt for France. As long as he could, Madison had clung to the idea that the Americans and French shared a common faith in mankind's capacity for self-government. While hoping that France would not revert to monarchy, he had to concede, as he wrote Jefferson in February 1800, that "melancholy evidence appears that the destiny of the revolution is transferred from the civil to the military authority." Weeks later, he lamented that "the late defection of France has left America the only theatre on which true liberty can have a fair trial."

Reluctant as they were to admit that the Federalists had proved better judges of the French Revolution, Jefferson and Madison were at last free to think of France as simply another European power. Now they could evaluate its policies toward America not in the exalted terms of the international struggle for liberty, but in the concrete language of national interest. Madison had never disputed the central definition of that interest that Washington had offered in his Farewell Address of 1796. "The great rule of conduct for us, in regard to foreign nations," the first President had declared (in words penned by Hamilton), "is in extending our commercial relations to have with them as little *political* connection as possible." Madison and Jefferson had disagreed with Hamilton not about the importance of commerce to American prosperity, but rather over the specific policies that the United States ought to pursue. Even freed from their sentimental attachment to France, the Republican leaders still believed that Great Britain posed the greatest threat to the development of an autonomous national economy.

The Republicans defined American economic and political interests in terms that reflected the agrarian society in which Madison and Jefferson had been reared. In their ideal world, the United States would remain a nation of productive farmers exporting bountiful surpluses to Europe and the West Indies in exchange for manufactured goods. Such an economy would support a sizable class of artisans who could make ships and houses, plows and barrels, cabinets and nails, and it would certainly need both merchants and merchantmen to carry American exports overseas. It should also sustain enough of a manufacturing base to minimize American dependence on British goods. But it would not require the kind of proletariat already found in the manufacturing towns of northern England or the masses of urban poor whom Jefferson had seen in Paris and London. Wage labor and urban life would sap the manly independence of the republic's citizens.

Madison subscribed fully to the romantic image of rural life that Jefferson had etched in his *Notes on the State of Virginia* when he declared that God had made the self-sufficient farmer "his peculiar deposit for substantial and genuine virtue." Since the 1780s, he had worried that population growth would create a restless underclass "of those who will labor under all the hardships of life, and secretly sigh for a more equal distribution of its blessings." Madison assumed that the "best distribution" of citizens was one that would allow most Americans to remain farmers. "The greater the proportion of this class to the whole society," he wrote in 1792, "the more free, the more independent, and the more happy must be the society itself."

Yet precisely because American farmers were not the battered peasantry whom Jefferson had met in his walks through France, the Republicans recognized the advantages of a modern dynamic economy. They were prophets of economic growth, not stagnation. American farmers wanted foreign markets for their surplus and land for their children, so that the next generation would enjoy the same prosperity as their parents. Both concerns came into play in the negotiations that led to the greatest foreign policy coup of the Jefferson presidency: the purchase of the Louisiana Territory from France in 1803.

Madison barely had time to learn the names of the half dozen clerks who made up the Department of State before a dispatch from Rufus King, the American minister to Britain, confirmed what had been rumored for some time: that Spain had secretly agreed to return Louisiana to its original sovereign, France. Madison promptly informed Louis Pichon, the French *chargé*, that this retrocession would lead to recurring conflict between the two countries. The United States could live with continued Spanish rule over Louisiana, but French control could only mean that Napoleon hoped to restore a French empire in North America.

While Spain delayed the formal transfer to France, the future of Louisiana came to hinge on another Napoleonic stroke. In 1802 Napoleon sent an expedition to reconquer the island of Santo Domingo, the scene of a bloody slave insurrection led by Toussaint L'Ouverture. Precisely because that revolt sent waves of fear pulsing through the Republican slaveholders of the South, Jefferson and Madison let Pichon know that they would not oppose the retaking of the island. But the ex-slaves' guerrilla tactics and yellow fever ravaged the expedition. News of its losses reached Napolean early in 1803. Soon he learned that a second expedition—this one destined for the occupation of Louisiana—would also be unable to complete its mission. A bitter winter had kept its ships frozen in their harbor in Holland. With relations with Britain rapidly worsening, Napolean could no longer risk sending the necessary troops to America.

These reverses made the First Consul suddenly receptive to the milder solution that Jefferson and Madison had proposed by extending an offer to purchase New Orleans and West Florida. Spanish authorities meanwhile had again barred Americans from depositing goods at New Orleans for transshipment into the Gulf of Mexico. Americans believed, wrongly, that France lay behind this maneuver. With calls for war echoing through the land, the administration sent James Monroe, its diplomatic troubleshooter, as a special envoy to France and Spain. When he reached Paris in April 1803, Monroe was astonished to learn that Napoleon was willing to put not only New Orleans but the entire Louisiana Territory on the table. Within weeks, at a net cost of $15 million, the United States obtained title to 828,000 square miles of land stretching northwest from the mouth of the Mississippi.

Back in Washington, Jefferson and Madison were happily stunned by the news. The President worried, though, whether the purchase was constitutional. Since the Constitution said nothing about the power of the federal government to obtain foreign territory, the theory of strict construction that the Republicans had repeatedly deployed against the Federalists might also be used to deny the validity of the purchase. Madison helped to still this overly scrupulous objection by arguing that the treaty clause of the Constitution provided all the authority needed to conclude an agreement so obviously in the national interest. If the President felt, however, that the later admission of the new territory into the union of the *states* required a constitutional amendment, he would accede to Jefferson's concerns.

Madison was equally firm when it came to a second obstacle to the purchase. In his eagerness to unload Louisiana, Napoleon had not bothered to consult the wishes of Spain, which might have kept the territory as a buffer protecting Mexico from the rising power to the north. But when the Spanish minister to America, the Marquis de Casa Yrujo, complained that the purchase violated the terms of the prior retrocession, Madison rejected his protest unequivocally, "giving him to understand," he wrote Monroe, "that we shall not withhold any means that may be rendered necessary to secure our object." Jefferson and the rest of the cabinet agreed. Rather than delay the sale to placate Spain, they agreed that the United States should be prepared to take "forcible possession of New Orleans"—though this proved unnecessary.

The Louisiana Purchase, the great achievement of Jefferson's first term, doubled the land mass of the United States and proved that the Republicans were prepared to act vigorously in pursuit of the national interest. The administration had no immediate plans to settle the vast territory west of the Mississippi. New states might arise there eventually, but it seemed more likely that this land would long be reserved for Indian nations already being driven off ancestral lands by the spread of settlement east of the Mississippi. For twenty years, Madison had worried that these settlers might abandon their loyalty to the original American union if it failed to gain free access to the markets their produce could reach only by being shipped down the Ohio and Mississippi rivers into the Gulf of Mexico. In this sense, New Orleans was the jewel in the crown. With good reason, then, the Republicans in Washington celebrated the news that the American flag had been raised over the city on December 20, 1803.

The administration hoped that Napoleon would include West Florida in the sale, but the newly self-proclaimed emperor denied that Florida was his to sell. In early 1804, Madison pressed the issue with the resentful Yrujo, while Monroe and

Charles Pinckney went to Madrid to negotiate directly with Spain. The efforts were futile. Spain refused to yield.

Madison was in Philadelphia—where Dolley had gone to seek treatment for a tumor on her leg—when Jefferson wrote to ask whether the United States should ally itself with Britain in order to secure Florida. Since Britain and France had gone back to war two years earlier, this proposal revealed how far the President had moved from his previous loyalty to France—and how large Florida loomed in his thinking. In theory, Madison wrote back, "an eventual alliance with G. B., if attainable from her without inadmissible conditions, would be for us the best of all possible measures." But he suspected that Britain would ask too high a price to make the bargain worthwhile. The "reciprocal engagement" Britain would seek, Madison replied on August 20, "would put us at once into the war"—exactly the last place that either man wanted the nation to find itself.

Madison was anxious to preserve the Anglo-American accommodation that the administration had inherited from John Adams. He responded quickly to the renewal of the Anglo-French war in May 1803 by sending Monroe, fresh from the Louisiana negotiations, to London to propose a treaty that Madison hoped would "put an end to every danger to which the harmony between the two countries is now subjected." Two sets of issues stood out as critical.

The first involved the practice of impressment. To meet its urgent need for seamen, the Royal Navy did not hesitate to stop American ships on the high seas or in foreign harbors, searching not only for deserters from its own men-of-war, but also for any British-born sailors who, under English law, remained subjects of George III and thus liable to armed service. Madison conceded that deserters might have to go unprotected. But to let the Royal Navy search American ships at will or snatch civilian sailors who had freely chosen the American flag was more than an independent republic could accept. The impressment issue thus had a symbolic importance that the administration could simply not ignore.

The second set of issues Madison wanted to resolve concerned the complex subject of neutral rights. Americans believed that a blockade had to be effective to be legal; it was not enough for Britain (or later France) to declare a paper blockade on harbors that its far-flung navy could not in fact patrol. A second issue concerned the legal definition of contraband. Assuming a blockade was effective, what goods could the enforcing power properly confiscate: military materiel alone, or other supplies that might prove vital to the economy of a blockaded country—especially the foodstuffs that comprised the bulk of American exports?

The thorniest questions of all involved the carrying trade with European colonies in the New World. American ships had been excluded from that trade in peacetime; but with the Royal Navy in control of the Atlantic, France and Spain had opened it to American ships. Britain had originally resisted this development under the so-called Rule of 1756, which held that trade closed to a neutral nation in peace could not be opened in time of war. But after 1794, the British doctrine of the broken voyage allowed an American ship to load a cargo in (say) Martinique, carry it to an American harbor, unload part of it and take on new goods, and then sail to Europe. The potential for abusing this trade was as enormous as the profits it offered, but until 1805, the British accepted the principle that "free ships make free goods."

The horrific Napoleonic Wars of 1803–1815 hardly provided an ideal testing ground for the broad claims of neutral rights that Jefferson and Madison favored. But the two men did not naively suppose that reason alone would vindicate their position. Instead they presumed that American markets and exports were so vital to both Britain and France that the belligerents would rather accept the administration's claims than risk American retaliation.

This idea of European dependence on America had played a critical role in the conduct of colonial resistance to Britain before 1776. And after the Revolution, Madison and Jefferson argued that only through commercial retaliation could the United States counter the restrictions other nations had placed on its shipping. Hamilton and his allies disagreed, and a frustrated Madison had watched the Federalists prefer accommodation to retaliation. But with Congress in Republican control and the war driving American trade with Europe to record levels, a fair test of retaliation was becoming more likely.

Still, Madison hoped to avoid confrontation, even after Monroe's discussions of 1804 proved futile. But by August 1805, he was ready for a more radical step. "If a commercial weapon can be properly shaped for the Executive hand," he wrote Jefferson in mid-September, "it is more and more apparent to me that it can force all the nations having colonies in this quarter of the globe, to respect our rights."

Madison was reacting to mounting evidence that Britain was ready to restrict the American carrying trade with the neutral islands of the West Indies. In the spring of 1805, two British courts had issued opinions signaling the new policy. Madison's response to these developments was decidedly academic. While Dolley took three months to recuperate in Philadelphia, Madison busied himself preparing a pamphlet on the whole subject.

The resulting treatise was presented to Congress in January 1806. Though unsigned, *An Examination of the British Doctrine, Which Subjects to Capture a Neutral Trade, Not Open in Time of Peace* was at once recognized as Madison's work. Its exhausting survey of relevant legal authorities bore the marks of his learned style. It also bored most of the congressmen who tried to wade through it. Whatever its academic merits, the *Examination* seemed a feeble response to a worsening situation. News that the Rule of 1756 had been reaffirmed in the *Essex* case had already sparked a furious debate that split Republicans in Congress into two factions. For while northern commercial interests, now well represented in the party, favored vigorous measures, southern Republicans were more cautious. The profits of the carrying trade meant little to their constituents, who would be satisfied if Britain allowed American exports of cotton, rice, tobacco, and wheat to go unmolested.

The course of debate in Congress revealed crucial political weaknesses in the administration's position. Jefferson had been easily reelected to a second term, the Republicans controlled both houses of Congress, and Alexander Hamilton had been killed by former Vice President Aaron Burr in their famous duel. All this freed the Republicans to air their differences with each other. "The Republicans," Madison wrote Monroe, "having lost the cement given to their union by the rivalship of the Federal party, have fallen in many places into schisms." In Congress, three factions fought for months over the importance of the carrying trade, the wisdom of barring the importation of British goods, and the President's request for a secret appropriation to purchase Florida. Madison and his pamphlet became the particular target of abuse from John Randolph of Virginia, the brilliant but wild leader of a small faction who accused both Jefferson and Madison of betraying true Republican principles.

The upshot of this debate was the adoption of a limited Nonimportation Act which would not take effect for nine months—time enough to renew negotiations with Britain. To this end, William Pinkney, a Maryland lawyer who had served on one of the arbitration commissions established by the Jay Treaty, was sent to join Monroe with fresh instructions from Madison. The envoys were to insist that Britain offer concessions on the continuance of the carrying trade and impressment on the high seas.

In fact the treaty that Monroe and Pinkney eventually signed on the last day of 1806 led Madison into a rift with Monroe that took several years to close. Monroe had wrongly taken Pinkney's appointment as a sign that he had lost Madison's confidence—perhaps because an overworked Madison had let his correspondence with Monroe lag. The modest concessions on the carrying trade and contraband that Britain offered in the treaty would operate only "during the present hostilities." In exchange, the United States renounced the use of commercial retaliation for ten years. On the key issue of impressment, Monroe and Pinkney obtained only a separate note vaguely stating that the Royal Navy would act with greater caution. Little progress was made on other issues relating to Anglo-American commerce.

Texts of the treaty reached Washington on March 3, 1807, just as Congress was adjourning. Madison immediately brought it to the President. Even in the grip of one of his recurring migraines, Jefferson needed only one reading to decide against submitting it to the Senate. Monroe defended the treaty for securing "as much as could reasonably have been expected," given that "the very existence" of Britain "depended on an adherence to its maritime pretensions." And that, as Jefferson and Madison saw it, was the rub. British "pretensions" were just that: arrogant claims that rested not on the law of nations or even prior practice or treaties, but on *"a mere superiority of force."*

That was the conclusion Madison had reached in researching the tangled questions of neutral rights. Whatever its literary flaws and political irrelevance, his *Examination* of the rule of 1756 had convinced Madison that much of British doctrine was intellectually bankrupt. This in turn confirmed his long-held opinion that the true purpose of British policy had not changed since 1783. It was still dedicated to stunting the growth of American commerce, especially the lucrative West Indian trade, and thus depriving the United States of the full benefits of independence. The humiliating practice of impressment was a product of the same arrogance. So long as British policy remained unchanged, the United States would be better advised to seek every commercial advantage it could, even those created by the temporary conditions of war.

Monroe's assessment of British policy was far sounder. Three years in Europe allowed him to grasp the nature of the Napoleonic challenge to Britain better than his superiors in Washington. With Admiral Nelson's victory at Trafalgar matched by Napoleon's triumph at Austerlitz, the war was a struggle between British mastery of the seas and French domination of the Continent. Far from making Britain vulnerable to American pressure, these events left it determined to maintain its naval and commercial supremacy at whatever cost.

Madison read the situation differently. He closed the new instructions he sent Monroe and Pinkney in March 1807 by listing the reasons why Britain was vulnerable to American pressure. The British West Indies depended on America for "the necessaries of life and of cultivation." The Royal Navy itself might seek vital stores from the United States if it lost its traditional sources of supply in the Baltic and Black seas. Nor should the British forget that American "granaries" could "supply the annual deficit of the British harvests." Against the danger that the United States might withhold all these "necessaries," Britain could only stop its exports to America—but such a step would hurt British workers and merchants far more than American consumers.

Within the administration, Madison had clearly emerged as the leading proponent of a hard line toward Britain. Such a tack became intensely popular after June 22, 1807, when the British man-of-war *Leopard*, without provocation, raked the American frigate *Chesapeake* with repeated broadsides, then boarded her and removed four "deserters"—three of them American citizens—from the shell-shocked crew. The fact that this vicious attack occurred within sight of the Virginia coast compounded the insult to American sovereignty.

The *Chesapeake* incident provided a sensational reminder of the festering danger of impressment. But a still graver challenge to American policy arose across the Atlantic. In his Berlin Decree of November 1806, Napoleon put the entire British Isles under blockade. In January Britain responded with Orders in Council prohibiting trade between any two continental ports—a common practice for American ships. Though neither navy could enforce these paper blockades consistently, numerous American merchantmen faced the threat of French and British confiscation. Both nations extended their restrictions later in the year. After Britain ordered all neutral vessels trading with Europe first to obtain a license in a British port, Napoleon's Milan Decree made all ships complying with this new rule also subject to seizure.

The administration responded to these developments in the late fall of 1807. War was out of the question. The Republicans' aversion to Hamiltonian schemes of finance had committed them to a program of reduced spending that had left the nation's forces in no state for combat. After finally allowing the twice-delayed Nonimportation Act of 1806 to take effect, the cabinet proposed a more radical step: the adoption of a law prohibiting American ships from trading with Europe. With little debate,

Congress approved this Embargo on December 22—too hastily to examine its implications seriously. It proved to be the most disastrous act of Jefferson's presidency.

While Jefferson viewed the Embargo as a means of preventing both war and the wholesale capture of American ships, Madison hoped that suspending commerce with the West Indies and Europe would finally force Britain and France to respect American neutrality. These differences betrayed a deeper failure to analyze the purpose and consequences of the Embargo. How long would it last? What should the United States do if the belligerents proved unyielding? How would the Embargo be enforced against merchants and shipowners who knew a thing or two about smuggling and the exploitation of legal loopholes—which the hastily drafted Embargo was soon enough found to contain?

Madison believed that resentment of both the *Chesapeake* incident and the general arrogance that both Britain and France displayed toward the United States would sustain popular support for the Embargo. By the summer of 1808, however, the liabilities were far more evident than the benefits. Hundreds of ships lay idle in American ports, and the merchants, seamen, artisans, and farmers who had prospered with the growth of maritime commerce since the 1790s suffered. Soon the administration had to mount thankless and futile efforts to enforce the Embargo against a restless citizenry—efforts that its critics thought no less oppressive than the Sedition Act of 1798. In coasting vessels and over northern lakes and roads, American produce flowed northward to Canada and from there to the West Indies, Britain, and Europe.

Britain's capacity to resist economic coercion far defied Madison's optimistic expectations. Prices rose, but enterprising merchants soon found new sources of supply—especially in Canada, which experienced a major boom not only through the illicit flow of goods from America but also in the produce of its own soil. And nothing that Madison learned from correspondents overseas suggested that either British or French policy would soon alter. By September 1808, he confessed to Jefferson that "we must . . . look to England alone for the chances of disembarrassment, and look with the greater solicitude, as it seems probable that nothing but some striking success of the Embargo can arrest the successful perversion of it by its enemies, or rather the enemies of their country."

The administration had never seriously considered what it would do if economic coercion failed. The congressmen who returned to Washington in December 1808 knew that the Embargo had to be either greatly strengthened or repealed. The Republican majority still looked to the White House for leadership. But in his final months in office, a dispirited Jefferson, pining for Monticello, insisted that he was only "a spectator," and that the initiative for revising policy should come from his successor.

That successor, everyone knew, would be James Madison. He had not been the unanimous choice of his party; sixty Republican congressmen boycotted the January 1808 caucus that gave Madison the party's nomination. Yet neither of his two rivals seriously challenged his candidacy. Governor George Clinton of New York was old and infirm, and Monroe, though allied with the Madison-baiting John Randolph, was reluctant to break with Jefferson, who supported Madison. Had the Embargo become law a year earlier, the backlash against it might have hurt Madison's chances within the party or against his Federalist opponent, Charles C. Pinckney. But many states had already voted before the full impact of the Embargo was felt. Seven years of Republican rule *before* the Embargo had reduced the Federalists to a disorganized opposition with only scattered strength outside New England. When Congress tallied the electoral votes in December 1808, Madison easily defeated Pinckney, 122–47.

Even as President-elect, Madison was reluctant to exercise authority that still properly belonged to Jefferson. Treasury secretary Albert Gallatin, who had carried the brunt of the difficult task of enforcing the Embargo, pushed the President to face the issue squarely. Convinced that commercial coercion had failed, Gallatin was at least willing to propose readying the country for war. Madison joined Gallatin in urging the President to act, and when Jefferson again balked, the two secretaries jointly prepared a report asking Congress to approve military preparations *and* the extension of the Embargo to include a broader program of commercial nonintercourse directed against Britain and France.

Yet when it came to finding the support needed to pass this program through a divided Congress, the President-elect failed his first test of leadership. Madison did little to influence the debate in Congress. Perhaps he felt there was nothing he could do to bring order out of the congressional chaos; in his lengthy experience he could think of "no occasion" when "the ideas" of Congress were "so unstable and so scattered." But he was hardly pleased by the Nonintercourse Act that Congress adopted in February. In theory, American trade with Britain and France was still barred. But in practice, simply by allowing long-confined American ships to clear harbor, the Act guaranteed both that they would resume trade with the belligerents and that many of them would fall prey to the restrictions that Britain and France still imposed on neutral commerce with the enemy.

The old Embargo expired on March 4, 1809—the day that James Madison took the oath of office as the fourth President of the United States.

CHAPTER FOURTEEN

Troubled Diplomacy

The inauguration took place twelve days short of Madison's fifty-eighth birthday. The new President delivered his inaugural address in the crowded chamber of the House of Representatives—but in a voice so low that listeners strained to hear his recital of the Republican creed. Observers at the evening celebrations thought he looked tired and subdued—especially when they cast their eyes from Madison over to Jefferson. Standing next to the gregarious, generously proportioned, and colorfully attired Dolley, the slim and reserved Madison, dressed in his customary black, hardly cut a commanding figure. Duty more than ambition had brought him to the presidency. The burdens of the past few years had taken their toll on his health. And the dispiriting results of the Embargo, both at home and abroad, suggested that he would enjoy no honeymoon at the start of his term.

Fortunately his marriage to Dolley had been—as it would remain—one long honeymoon of its own. Once moved in, Dolley immediately set about making the White House a suitable place for entertaining. Jefferson had used the quarters for small dinners where he would wine and dine his guests while conversing on an astonishing range of subjects. The Madisons gave Washington society a different tone by holding more elaborate functions at which Dolley excelled as a hostess. Like Jefferson, the new President believed that republican manners should be polite but informal, substituting American warmth and directness for the pretentious and rigid forms he associated with the Old World.

Madison faced serious political difficulties from the start. He did not enjoy the same personal loyalty and affection that Jefferson had gained during his two terms. Nor was his party the unified corps who had driven the Federalists from power eight years earlier. While resentment of the Embargo had allowed the Federalists to make a modest revival, the opposition remained a nuisance at worst, strong enough to make mischief in Congress, but too weak to force the Republicans to rally around their President in order to preserve their party's rule.

The first sign of trouble came with the formation of the cabinet. Madison had wanted Secretary of the Treasury Gallatin to take his own place at the State Department. It immediately became evident that the Swiss-born Gallatin had too many rivals and critics in his own party to be confirmed by the Senate. Madison kept Gallatin in his cabinet by simply allowing him to stay on at Treasury, where he remained the object of malicious criticism. But in Gallatin's intended place at State, Madison had to put the amiable but inept Robert Smith, the brother of Senator Samuel Smith of Maryland, a leading Gallatin foe. Madison thus sentenced himself to act as his own secretary of state. Other cabinet appointments went to placate the sectional factions of his party. Caesar Rodney of Delaware stayed on as attorney general; William Eustis of Massachusetts became secretary of war; Paul Hamilton of South Carolina took over the Navy Department and the decrepit fleet of gunboats that Jefferson wrongly thought could defend American coastal waters.

The overriding task was to sort out the diplomatic options in the aftermath of the Embargo. Prospects for accommodation with Britain suddenly improved in April 1809, when David Erskine, the British envoy since 1806, reported he had new instructions promising the revocation of the Orders of Council if the United States did not apply the Nonintercourse Act against Britain. In a brief flurry of negotiations, Madison and Robert

Smith reached agreement with Erskine, and on April 19 the President issued a proclamation permitting American trade with Britain after June 10. But in fact Erskine had defied his instructions on several crucial points that he knew Madison would never accept, and it took his government little time to repudiate the agreement.

Madison received the unexpected news at Montpelier in July. Until then he had dared to believe that the Embargo had actually worked. "The school of adversity," he wrote Jefferson, had taught Britain the wisdom of replacing her "arrogant pretensions" toward the United States with "a conciliating moderation." Hopefully the French, "if not bereft of common sense, or . . . predetermined on war with us," would follow suit. Now American commerce was once more exposed to the depredations of the belligerents. Summoned back to Washington by Gallatin, Madison and his cabinet again subjected Britain to the Nonintercourse Act. But hundreds of American ships had meanwhile made their way to British and West Indian ports, undercutting the restrictions the Act reimposed.

By the fall of 1809, the central problem of foreign policy was to fashion a strategy that would enable American merchantmen to trade directly with British and European markets. Since Britain had largely abandoned the Rule of 1756, the carrying trade with the West Indies had returned to its earlier footing. Impressment remained a symbolic sticking point, but in Madison's thinking, protecting the rights of individual sailors mattered far less than the wholesale threat to American prosperity posed by the rival blockades of Britain and France.

The alternatives Madison faced were hardly appealing. If the United States took a strong stand on neutral rights, it had to be willing to oppose the offensive policies of *both* belligerents. Even if Congress voted the sums required to ready the nation for armed conflict—which it seemed reluctant to do—the country could not risk war with Britain and France at the same time. But the very need to strengthen the armed forces threatened the nation's ability to pursue measures short of war. Prolonged commercial warfare with Britain would be costly, Gallatin reminded Madison; without receipts from duties on British imports, the government would operate at a deficit—a prospect that filled devout Republicans with terror.

Notwithstanding this problem, Madison clung to the belief that the best strategy was to couple economic coercion with forthright diplomacy. But from the start his inability to control his party compromised this policy. To some extent, Madison was a prisoner of his constitutional convictions. He did not believe—as had Hamilton—that the executive alone should set foreign policy, especially when the Constitution explicitly vested the power to regulate foreign commerce in Congress. This was a noble judgment in principle, but one that presented Madison with political and diplomatic problems. For his failure to persuade a fractious Congress to support his foreign policies not only exposed him to political embarrassment at home, it also undermined his complicated diplomatic strategies abroad.

The weakness of Madison's leadership became evident after the Eleventh Congress reassembled in November 1809. Acting for the administration, Nathaniel Macon introduced a bill, largely drafted by Gallatin, allowing American ships to sail freely to and from European harbors while prohibiting belligerent vessels from entering American waters. Macon's Bill #1, as it was called, met defeat at the hands of a coalition of Federalists and anti-Gallatin Republicans in the Senate. After further debates, Congress instead removed all restrictions on American trade while allowing the President to restore nonintercourse against one belligerent only after the other had voluntarily revoked its offensive edicts. Since the Royal Navy could prevent French ships from reaching American ports, and American vessels from reaching most European harbors, the new act (Macon's Bill #2, approved in May 1810) seemed to favor Britain—while still exposing American ships trading with Britain to capture by French privateers.

Madison's doubts about this measure must have been known in Congress. Yet he did not attempt to influence its debates, nor did he consider vetoing its decision. Like other early presidents, he regarded the veto as a weapon of self-defense, to be used not in disputes over policy but only if Congress trespassed on the duties of the executive. Madison's awareness of the divisions within his party reinforced his caution. "The Republicans, as usual, are either not decided, or have different leanings," he informed Jefferson early in the session, while "the Federalists are lying in wait to spring on any opportunity." With Congress in this "unhinged state" and public opinion opposed to renewing the Embargo, he remained a spectator to the deliberations.

For better or worse—Madison thought worse—Macon's Bill #2 defined the context within which he now had to conduct foreign policy. (The great duty of the President, after all, was to "take care that the laws be faithfully executed.") From the start, he assessed the potential consequences of the act coldly. Writing to William Pinkney on May 23, he predicted that Britain would have "a compleat interest in perpetuating" a state of affairs "which gives her the full enjoyment of our trade" while increasing the chance that the implicit American submission to British regulations would lead to hostilities between the United States and France. The one hope that Madison held out was that Napoleon would prefer "to turn the tables on G. Britain" by first revoking his edicts, thereby triggering American nonintercourse with Britain and "compelling her either to revoke her orders, or to lose the commerce of this country. An apprehension that France may take this politic course," Madison concluded, "would be a rational motive with the British Government to get the start of her" by repealing *its* edicts first.

But Madison doubted that this favorable turn of events would come to pass. He expected, rather, that both belligerents would show "increased obstinacy" toward the United States, and he hoped that this in turn would reverse "the passive spirit which marked the late session of Congress" and leave both the public and their representatives willing to resort to coercive measures.

In his mercurial fashion, Napoleon managed to meet several of Madison's expectations—but in a way that only aggravated the dilemma. As Madison had feared, the Emperor's first action was retaliatory: the Rambouillet decree of March 1810 ordered the seizure of all American ships in French harbors, regardless of whether they had complied with the British regulations. After learning of Macon's Act, however, Napoleon changed his mind. In early August he ordered his foreign minister, the Duke of Cadore, to inform John Armstrong, Jr., (the American minister to France) that the Milan and Berlin decrees would be void after November 1 if the British revoked their Orders in Council or if the United States "shall cause their rights to be respected by the English."

Napoleon thus turned the logic of Macon's Act against itself by forcing the United States to take action *before* his own new policy took effect. Madison's response to this gambit was delayed by a lack of solid information on which to act. He first learned of the French decision from reports in London newspapers—hardly an authoritative source. Madison's only evidence was a text of Cadore's August 5 letter to Armstrong, who proved unaccountably slow to explain what Napoleon was up to. Dispatches from Armstrong did not arrive until early November. By then Madison had already decided to exploit the French opening. On November 2 he issued a proclamation formally recognizing the repeal of the French decrees and further announcing that unless Britain removed its restrictions in turn, nonintercourse with Britain would resume in three months.

For Madison, this was quite a gamble. He understood the calculated ambiguity of the French declaration, and he knew from experience not to trust Napoleon. Yet rather than wait for clarification of French policy, Madison hoped that taking the Cadore letter at face value would induce Napoleon to honor its terms. France should want to deprive Britain of its access to American goods and markets. Moreover, while Madison regarded Britain and France as "equally distrustful," he believed that British enmity toward America was rooted in a commercial rivalry that ran deeper than the mere rapacity of Napoleon. Seizing the opening from France would also encourage Americans to focus their resentment against Britain, so that the United States would gain "the advantage at least of having but one contest on our hands at one time." With Congress soon due to reassemble, Madison may have hoped that early action on his part would prevent a repetition of the divisive debates of the last session.

These wishful calculations soon proved faulty. Madison was gratified when loyal congressmen secured the passage of a revised Nonintercourse Act directed against Britain. But he lost a crucial battle to recharter the Bank of the United States when Vice President George Clinton, a likely rival for the presidency in 1812, cast the deciding vote against it in the Senate. Madison had swallowed his consitutional objections against the Bank because Gallatin, the architect of Republican financial policy, insisted that its lending services would be needed to limit the taxes that Congress would otherwise have to levy to prepare the nation's armed forces for war.

Madison's efforts to extract concessions from Britain also proved futile. The British cabinet dismissed Napoleon's gambit as the snare Madison suspected it might be, and kept its Orders in Council in force. For his part, Napoleon continued to seize American vessels and to hold on to hundreds of others captured earlier, while imposing new restrictions on American ships trading directly with the continent. Negotiations with Britain were further hampered by the conduct of Secretary of State Smith, whose only loyalties lay to his senatorial brother. Smith even told the British chargé d'affaires that his government was right to resist the President's demands.

Madison had kept Smith in his cabinet only to maintain the facade of Republican unity. But in addition to their unceasing campaign against Gallatin, the Smith brothers now seemed bent on preventing Madison's renomination in 1812. Pressure from Gallatin finally forced Madison to act. After several bizarre interviews in March 1811—in which Smith declined a diplomatic posting to Russia and said he would rather fill a vacancy on the Supreme Court (though he had not practiced law for years)—Madison removed him from office. When Smith took his case to the public, his wild charges against Madison only discredited their accuser—but his portrait of a divided administration did little to bolster respect for the President's leadership.

In Smith's place, Madison named James Monroe. At the urging of Jefferson, the two men had revived their personal friendship the previous summer; both realized that political reconciliation would also serve their interests. Madison gained a competent secretary of state, while Monroe ended his self-imposed political exile and rejoined the Republican leadership. Most important, because Monroe had earlier sought to reach an accommodation with Britain, his presence in the cabinet would blunt criticism that Madison was blindly bent on forcing a confrontation with Britain.

But Monroe's appointment could not magically dissolve the dilemma in which Madison had already placed himself by accepting Napoleon's cunning offer. The failure of France to rescind its decrees in their full scope gave Britain a plausible pretext to argue that its Orders in Council should remain in force. When a new British minister, Sir John Foster, arrived in Washington in June 1811, he carried instructions that left little room for accommodation. Not only did Foster deny that France *was* now respecting neutral rights; he insisted that the Orders in Council could be revoked only if France both allowed American ships to carry British goods into European harbors and restored the rights of neutral commerce as they had been understood before the Milan and Berlin decrees took effect. If anything, the talks between Monroe and Foster indicated that the British position had grown more militant, and that it would likely remain so while the war continued. By August 1811, Madison concluded that "Foster seems more disposed to play the diplomatist, than the conciliatory negociator."

Diplomatic retreat or a resort to force are the usual solutions for the impasse Madison had reached as he returned to Montpelier in the late summer of 1811. He found the first alternative almost unthinkable. Had he shared Hamilton's view of the compatibility of American and British interests, he might have explained British obstinacy as the unavoidable result of the brutal struggle against Napoleon. But because his assessment of the true national interest had long run in exactly the opposite direction, he accepted the risk of confrontation with Britain while ignoring mounting evidence of the "crafty contrivance and insatiable cupidity" of Napoleon. If the country could not afford conflict with both belligerents, Britain remained the preferred foe. Yet Madison still hoped that Britain would back down once it saw Congress acting to prepare the nation for war. If Britain did not relent, he was willing to accept war as the only satisfactory alternative to a prolongation of the diplomatic impasse.

One other consideration made a resort to force more likely. The phenomenal development of Canada, spurred both by British needs and policy *and* the effects of the Embargo, shook Madison's confidence in the efficacy of economic coercion. Not only could Canada attract a substantial illegal trade from the United States, forcing the administration to adopt drastic measures against its own citizens, its production of timber for the Royal Navy and foodstuffs for the West Indies also threatened to reduce British dependence on American supplies. Although American supplies were still valued by Britain, the expansion of the Canadian economy was steadily enhancing Britain's ability to withstand whatever forms of economic pressure the United States could exert. Conceivably the development of Canada could even affect the loyalties of many northern farmers, who could hardly ignore the vitality of the Canadian market—or the attractiveness of Canadian land to emigrants seeking a better stake.

Madison returned to Washington in October 1811 to prepare for the opening session of the Twelfth Congress. His annual message of November 5 asked Congress to initiate a series of measures to ready the nation for armed conflict with Britain. Though Gallatin—ever concerned about the costs of financing a war—managed to moderate this message, Congress seemed receptive. Its membership included a number of vocal new representatives from the western states who had barely read the President's message before news reached the capital of an armed Indian rising in the Northwest Territory. Many Americans suspected that the British in Canada were behind the rising. They were wrong: the native tribes were rallying not to the Union Jack but to the call of the messianic Shawnee Prophet and his warrior brother, Tecumseh. But the suspicion that the uprising was directed from Canada fostered increased animosity against Britain.

Discontent with the diplomacy of the past five years guaranteed that Congress would not balk at the idea of war. But public resentment of Britain could not erase the recurring problems that dogged all Madison's dealings with Congress. The more Congress considered the details of preparedness, the more it moved away from the administration's recommendations. Madison's chief Republican critics argued that his plans did not go far enough, and more loyal members of his party grew restive over the costs of preparedness. Ignoring objections from both the House and the administration, the Senate insisted on expanding the army to 25,000 regulars, enlisted for five years. Such a force was more than the country could realistically raise or even use, especially if, as Madison planned, the best American strategy would be to mount an early invasion of Canada, "before the enemy would be prepared to resist its progress." Moreover, its projected expense gave Congress a reason to avoid building the additional frigates needed to challenge the Royal Navy.

While Monroe and Gallatin presented the administration's views, Madison remained aloof from the debates in Congress. Privately he feared that its inconsistent acts demonstrated only that the United States was not ready for war—thus undermining the hope for a belated reversal of British policy. But by the early spring of 1812, a Congress restless from its prolonged session needed guidance. On March 31, Monroe told the House Committee on Foreign Affairs that the President believed "that without an accommodation with Great Britain, Congress ought to declare war before adjourning." No decision should be taken, Monroe added, until the sloop *Hornet* returned from Europe with the latest diplomatic dispatches. Meanwhile, to bring additional pressure to bear on Britain, whose army in the Iberian Peninsula was currently being fed with American grain, the administration asked Congress to approve a new Embargo for sixty days.

Although skeptical and impatient congressmen thought that Madison still hoped to evade war, his hesitation reflected his desire to have some definitive news on which to propose a formal declaration. April and May 1812 were months of nervous waiting, until at last the *Hornet* arrived on May 22. The news it carried lacked the dramatic quality Madison sought. From

France, minister Joel Barlow reported little change in Napoleon's position. From Britain, minister Jonathan Russell reported that the Orders in Council were still in effect, though under heavy attack from merchants and manufacturers, whose sufferings from the general economic depression that had begun in 1810 had been compounded by the nonintercourse that Congress had restored in 1811.

Madison had hoped that the news from Europe would convince the whole nation of the justice of a war with Britain. Instead, the failure of France to allow the administration to place on Britain the entire onus for the violation of American rights made the situation "more than ever puzzling," Madison wrote Jefferson on May 25. "To go to war with Britain and not with France arms the Federalists with new matter, and divides the Republicans, some of whom" still preferred "a display of impartiality." But with scores of congressmen ready to bolt for home, the time for hesitation had passed. At some point before May 29, a group of Republican congressmen led by Speaker of the House Henry Clay visited the White House and apparently insisted on action.

The President complied. On June 1, Madison sent Congress his war message. After reviewing the multiple grievances against Britain—including impressment and the Indian war in the west as well as the wholesale violations of neutral rights—Madison asked Congress for its declaration of war. Action against France could be suspended until "unclosed discussions" with that nation were completed. On June 4, the House approved the declaration of war by a vote of 79–40, but it took the Senate until the 17th to do the same, and only then by the narrow margin of 19–13. An exhausted Madison added his signature to the declaration on the 18th.

Five days later, the British cabinet suspended its Orders in Council. Had it acted two months earlier, war might have been avoided. But after years of futile diplomacy and confused politics, most Americans as well as their elected officials were almost relieved to find themselves at war—especially a conflict that many regarded as a second war of independence.

CHAPTER FIFTEEN

From Defeat, Victory

Dissident Republicans as well as Federalists had hoped that Madison's difficulties in dealing with Congress, Great Britain, and France would prevent his reelection. On May 18, 1812, the Republican congressional caucus renominated Madison by a unanimous vote of 82–0—though one-third of the caucus members boycotted the meeting. De Witt Clinton, the Republican governor of New York, was the rival candidate in the place of his uncle, Vice President George Clinton, who had died in mid-April. Rather than offer their own candidate, the Federalists, now confined almost entirely to New England, supported Clinton. The New Yorker carried his own state and all of New England except Vermont, but Madison, without campaigning, won reelection by a margin of 128–29 in the electoral college.

War dominated Madison's activities during the final months of his first term and the first half of his second. This marked the most trying passage of his long political career. There was blame enough to go around for the sorry character of the nation's war effort: from divisions in the cabinet and Congress to the rank incompetence of much of the officer corps, as well as the virulent hostility that made New England at best a neutral party to the conflict. But as President, commander-in-chief, and the chief architect of foreign policy, no one bore greater responsibility than Madison.

The war, after all, was the outcome of his policy. If events found Americans unable to meet its demands, he would have been better advised to stick to the path of diplomacy, however thankless it seemed. Once declared, war made the President peculiarly responsible for the national welfare. For as Madison well knew, the creation of the executive office had been much the result of the framers' desire to provide more efficient wartime leadership than the Continental Congress had offered during the Revolution. Indeed, if one of the central concerns of 1787 had been to improve the nation's capacity to wage war, then the experience of the War of 1812 seemed to suggest that the Constitution itself was a failure. In theory, the Constitution had freed the new national government from its dependence on the states. But in practice, the War of 1812 found the federal government nearly as dependent on the states as the Continental Congress had been during the Revolution.

The deeper difficulties that Madison faced, however, involved politics and policies, men and measures, and American ideas about war itself. Several broad factors help to explain the lackluster war effort. The armed forces were ill-prepared for conflict. Since the 1790s, the Republicans had been committed to a policy of retiring the national debt and avoiding new taxes—especially those used to build up an army and navy that they regarded as unproductive drains on the public treasury. On these matters, treasury secretary Gallatin was the truest Republican of all. To keep the budget in balance, Gallatin had repeatedly insisted on holding military expenditures within prudent bounds. Congress happily complied. So long as Madison was content to pursue measures short of war, few congressmen would support the taxes and loans that any serious effort at preparedness required. Even when war was declared, Gallatin hoped it could be fought as cheaply as possible. This commitment to economy crippled efforts to recruit men and collect supplies.

Finding capable leadership was even more challenging. Nearly twenty years had passed since the Indian wars of the 1790s. Few aging revolutionary officers were ready (mentally or physically) for combat, and many proved incompetent. Political ambition and petty claims of honor infected every level of command; officers resigned at the slightest insult. Although Madison had well-defined ideas of the strategy he wanted to pursue, he did not think himself competent to direct the war, a task better entrusted to the respective secretaries of the army and navy departments. But neither of the current holders of those offices merited great confidence. Secretary of the Army William Eustis was at best an overqualified clerk, while Secretary of the Navy Hamilton, a drunkard, could not stay awake past noon. Madison soon replaced Eustis with John Armstrong, former envoy to France and a revolutionary veteran who proved less interested in giving adequate direction to the war than in promoting his own prospects to succeed Madison in the presidency, which put him in perpetual competition with Secretary of State Monroe. More successful was Madison's appointment of William Jones as secretary of the navy.

Without popular confidence in either political or military leadership, Madison knew, the task of mobilizing the country would grow even more difficult. Even with it, there seemed to be little hope of bringing New England into the war. Federalist-dominated state governments there obstructed recruiting efforts while preventing their own militias from joining the crucial campaigns in neighboring Canada.

Nor could public support for the war be taken for granted even outside New England. Most Republicans had welcomed the decision for war because it promised to end years of futile diplomacy and fruitless attempts at economic coercion. But that attitude would not long survive defeat on the battlefield. Nor did the British revocation of the Orders in Council help the cause much. Why pursue the war at all, skeptics wondered, if Britain seemed willing to respond to America's major complaints, however belatedly? Indeed, as evidence of Napoleon's duplicity mounted, accompanied by news of his disastrous retreat from Russia, Federalist criticism grew more valid.

There was, finally, the question of presidential leadership itself. Rather than abandon long-held fears about the dangers of executive power, Madison hoped to demonstrate that a president could lead the republic into war without becoming a dictator. The administration, of course, would make its plans and wishes known to Congress, but ultimately the lawmakers had to decide how to raise and arm men and meet the costs of war. But Madison was no more master of Congress after 1812 than he had been in his first term. With the Republican party itself a fractious coalition, and the Federalists in Congress opposed to the war entirely, nearly every measure became the subject of heated debate. Even the most vigorous presidential leadership would not have brought instant harmony and consensus to Congress. But the idea that a President should seek to direct the debates of Congress was something that Madison had never come to accept.

Madison pinned his hopes for the war on prompt and decisive action against Canada, ideally through a three-pronged offensive aimed at holding everything from Montreal southwest to Detroit. Such a campaign might deter the British from attacking the United States and reduce the danger from Indian assaults on settlements in the Ohio Valley. But Madison also saw the occupation of Canada as the logical extension of his cherished belief that Britain would treat the United States fairly only if threatened with the loss of access to the resources of North America. Thus a war launched to secure American rights on the high seas came to depend on the success of military expeditions against the thinly peopled settlements of Canada. Equally important, early victories in Canada would provide the best and perhaps the only means to rally public opinion—even in New England—behind the war.

Within weeks of the declaration of war, these hopes were exposed as impracticable. The first campaign of 1812 brought one disappointment after another. As Madison feared, Congress's plan for a 25,000-man army proved too ambitious. Recruiting and the collection of supplies ran far behind schedule. Where adequate numbers of American troops, often poorly trained, were in the field, they were commanded by generals who were overly cautious at best and downright incompetent at worst. As early as August 16, General William Hull surrendered the fort at Detroit and an army of 2,000 men to an inferior British force without even firing a shot. A large force of Ohio and

Kentucky militia, commanded by William Henry Harrison, governor of the Indiana territory, made no attempt to retake Detroit, much less invade Upper Canada. Further east, General Henry Dearborn proved equally timid. After failing to secure any support in New England, Dearborn was unwilling to carry out his assigned task of launching an assault against Montreal.

The campaign of 1813 fared modestly better, but still fell far short of military or diplomatic success. Britain had now begun to reinforce its forces in Canada. With the war in Europe rapidly turning against Napoleon, there seemed ever less chance that the American army, still undermanned, ill-equipped, and poorly led, could gain a decisive victory beyond its border. In the fall of 1813, after Commodore Oliver Perry had cleared Lake Erie of British ships, Harrison defeated a British force at the Thames River in Ontario, thereby securing the northwestern settlements against attack. But Montreal, which Madison regarded as the great objective, still lay beyond the reach of the army. Moreover, the Royal Navy effectively blockaded American ports from New York south, while leaving the trade of New England open in the plausible hope of promoting disunion.

Even amid these disappointments, Madison analyzed the sources of his problems with dispassion. Without seeking "to shun whatever blame may be justly chargeable on the executive," he privately ascribed to Congress the key decisions that had made it impossible to put an adequate army in the field. While the new House of Representatives that met in May 1813 proved far more supportive than its predecessor, the Senate remained a harsh testing ground on almost every measure. Whether Madison faulted himself for weak leadership *within* the administration is more difficult to determine. Other than Gallatin and Monroe, the President's subordinates were a lackluster group. The Republican party, for all its political strengths, had produced few notable men of administrative talent. Too often, as in the appointment of Armstrong as secretary of war, the choice seemed to lie between greater and lesser degrees of incompetence. Madison might have turned to the party's new leaders in Congress—men like Henry Clay of Kentucky, John C.

Calhoun of South Carolina, or William Crawford of Georgia. Given his recurring problems with Congress, however, Madison could not afford to remove able supporters from the other end of Pennsylvania Avenue.

But the deepest difficulties facing Madison stemmed from the risky assumptions of his own policy. Once American arms failed to gain the early victories he had counted on, the odds of bringing the war to a successful conclusion declined almost monthly. With the French position in Europe collapsing, the British could reinforce Canada with battle-hardened troops from the Duke of Wellington's armies. More than that, the prospective end of the European war threatened to nullify the entire purpose of the conflict with Britain. For if peace came to Europe, neutral rights and impressment—to which Madison gave new emphasis after the revocation of the Orders in Council—would become irrelevant. Madison could hardly sustain the war to secure an abstract commitment protecting American rights in the event of some future conflict.

Opportunities to end the war by diplomacy had existed from the moment it was declared. The British minister in Washington, John Augustus Foster, had immediately asked Madison to suspend hostilities to give his government time to respond to a development it obviously had not foreseen. While indicating that negotiations were welcome, Madison had rejected that request, precisely because time was the last thing he could offer Britain if the United States were to gain the upper hand in the war.

By the winter of 1813, however, Madison could not afford to be so optimistic. Thus in February he accepted Tsar Alexander's offer to mediate an end to the conflict. Madison nominated Gallatin and James A. Bayard, a respected Federalist senator from Delaware, to join John Quincy Adams, the American minister to Russia, for the negotiation. But the Senate, still the home of Gallatin's most adamant critics, refused to go along unless the treasury secretary left the cabinet. In June 1813, after Gallatin had already arrived in St. Petersburg—and with Madison still recovering from a near-fatal bout of his "bilious indisposition" (perhaps malarial fever)—the Senate rejected the nomination by a single vote.

Rather than accept the Tsar's mediation, Britain proposed to open direct negotiations with the United States. Madison again immediately decided to accept this initiative, ignoring the objections of Secretary of War Armstrong, who feared it would detract from his own preparations for the campaign of 1814. To this peace commission, Madison again nominated Gallatin (who had by now resigned his cabinet post), Adams, and Bayard, along with Henry Clay and Jonathan Russell, former minister to France.

Madison knew that much of the campaign of 1814 would be fought before any results—good or bad—could be heard from the negotiations. His expectations could not have been great, in part because his confidence in Armstrong, never high to begin with, was steadily reduced by the secretary's clashes with Congress, by his evident political rivalry with Monroe, and also by evidence that Armstrong was ignoring Madison's instructions and keeping the president uninformed about the state of the army. Madison believed that cabinet heads should have a substantial degree of independence—but Armstrong was close to crossing the line between independence and insubordination. In August 1814, Madison was finally driven to give Armstrong a formal written lesson distinguishing routine administrative details and the more important decisions that required presidential knowledge or approval.

Almost immediately Madison found reason to regret his failure to impose his authority on his petulant secretary of war much earlier. Since June he had feared that British forces, which had been mounting raids all along the American coast, might attack Washington. Armstrong thought Baltimore a more likely target, and he ignored Madison's orders to prepare the defense of the capital. That task was left to another incompetent, General William Winder, who acted the part of a headless chicken even before a substantial British force appeared at the mouth of the Patuxent River, thirty-five miles southeast of Washington, on August 17.

While Dolley busied herself saving as much as she could of the White House papers and furnishings, Madison and Monroe (who had served in the Revolution under Washington) mounted a belated effort to organize effective opposition. Though the available troops outnumbered the enemy, the defense of the capital rested almost entirely on untried militia. At the battle of Bladensburg on August 24, Madison, mounted on horseback and packing a pair of dueling pistols, watched as the militia repeatedly broke before a disciplined British attack. Madison then rode back to the White House, which he found deserted, and on to the Virginia side of the Potomac. Behind him much of the capital lay in flames. When he finally returned to Washington late on August 27, he found both the White House and the Capitol gutted and burned. Given that he had spent the better part of a week on horseback, at a time of the year when his constitution was usually at its weakest, the sixty-three-year-old Madison weathered these events remarkably well. Privately, however, Madison must have faulted himself for not replacing Armstrong sooner, or at least for having failed to order the secretary to undertake the defensive measures that Madison had rightly judged were necessary.

In the crisis, Armstrong had proved worse than useless. After a blunt conversation in which Madison detailed his failings, the secretary of war resigned, to be replaced by Monroe. But popular disgust with Armstrong's performance deflected only a fraction of the general criticism directed against Madison's conduct of the war. Luckily for the President and the country, the burning of Washington was more of a political embarrassment than a military disaster, and even more luckily, two notable successes followed in mid-September. American forces at Baltimore held out against the bombardment of Fort McHenry, while far to the north, a naval victory on Lake Champlain allowed New York and Vermont militia to repel a British army intended for Albany.

Neither victory, however, brought the war any nearer to a successful conclusion. The administration itself was in disarray. Monroe remained acting head of his old department as well as secretary of the army. And without Gallatin at the treasury, there was no one capable of proposing ways and means to rescue the government from the financial crisis to which its declining credit and revenues had brought it. When nervous congressmen returned to the capital in late September, Madison was unprepared to explain how the war could be carried on into the new year. Even after he replaced Gallatin's unqualified successor, George W. Campbell, with the more respected Alexander Dallas, disputes within the administration and with Congress left the war effort in its usual uncertain state.

Nor did news from Europe offer grounds for hope. Dispatches from the peace commission at Ghent reached Washington in early October, revealing that Britain was seeking a victor's peace that would exclude American fishermen from Canadian waters, alter American boundaries, and protect Britain's Indian allies against future American expansion. The five American envoys had rejected these terms out of hand—but that left open the possibility, Madison informed Jefferson, that they might leave Ghent and accept "an indignant rupture of the negotiations."

A confirmed Anglophobe, Madison was never surprised by the harsh tenor of British policy toward the United States. What did disturb him was the idea that Britain had been sustained largely by New England's refusal to aid the war effort. "The conduct of the eastern states," he complained in November, was "the source of our greatest difficulties in carrying on the war, as it certainly is the greatest, if not the sole inducement with the enemy to persevere in it." From the outset, he had rested his hopes for a just peace on "convinc[ing] the enemy that he has to contend with the whole and not a part of the nation." But with delegates from Connecticut, Massachusetts, and Rhode Island due to meet in December at a special convention in Hartford, Madison feared that Federalist extremists might be plotting secession.

The one source of encouragement was the course of the naval war against Britain. On the high seas, the navy's newly built and powerful frigates had engaged in a number of successful combats against British men-of-war. These ships and scores of privateers had also captured or sunk over thirteen hundred merchantmen. These losses evoked strong protests from British merchants against continuing the war for uncertain territorial gains—which, in any case, American victories on northern lakes had rendered less likely.

Whether this was enough to bring Britain to make peace was more than Madison could yet know. In poor health during the fall of 1814, he was further distressed by the sudden death of Vice President Elbridge Gerry. Madison played the stoic as best he could. But as the new year approached, he sensed that the fate of the republic hinged on events he could neither control nor even influence. His thoughts were fastened on two distant cities. One, of course, was Ghent; the other was New Orleans, whose capture he knew to be the object of a substantial expedition sent out from Britain.

The anxiously awaited news from the southwest arrived first. On February 4, Madison and everyone else in Washington learned of Major General Andrew Jackson's astounding repulse of the British assault toward New Orleans, a victory that ruled out whatever possibility existed that Britain would gain control of the vital city that Madison and Jefferson had struggled so long to obtain. Ten days later came copies of the peace treaty that the American commissioners had signed at Ghent on Christmas Eve. The treaty left the original causes of war—neutral rights and impressment—unmentioned; but the end of the general war in Europe had already made those issues moot. More important, the treaty included none of the threatening terms that the British had first proposed. The territorial integrity of the nation was preserved, and Anglo-American relations returned, in effect, to the *status quo ante bellum*—realistically, the best the United States could obtain. Having reconciled himself to ending the war on this basis, Madison immediately sent the treaty on to the Senate, which took less than a day to ratify it unanimously. Among the few observers who could not wholeheartedly join the celebrations that immediately followed were the three delegates from the Hartford Convention who had just come to Washington to express New England's undiminished opposition to the war.

However many weaknesses the War of 1812 had exposed in the American political and constitutional system, and more to the point, in the foreign policy and administrative abilities of the President, Madison could at least be consoled that the war had come to a miraculously satisfactory end. Both the Constitution and the Union had been sorely tried. Congress had hardly acted the part of disinterested legislature, deliberating wisely on the common good. Madison had presided over an executive branch plagued by divided counsels and administrative inexperience. The federal government as a whole had been forced to rely on the state governments to carry out many of its measures; but if anything, the states had proved more deficient in this respect than they had been during the worst period of the Revolution a quarter century earlier.

Yet for all this, the Union had survived—and that may have been the one result of the War of 1812 that finally mattered most. But the President may have found another lesson in the outcome of the conflict. His conduct of the war had been more principled than pragmatic. But to Madison, the greatest challenge that any republic could meet in time of war was to preserve its principles against all the expedient concerns that could justify their violation. On that score, the government of the United States had come through a difficult struggle in much better shape than its critics or even its friends had suspected it could.

CHAPTER SIXTEEN

Outliving Himself

Entering the seventh year of his presidency in 1815, Madison could at last turn his attention to domestic concerns—both the nation's and his own. For nearly a decade and a half, foreign and military affairs had occupied his attention. Since 1811 he had managed to spend only a few months at Montpelier. At Washington he found the burdens of office inescapable. Often he worked by candle nearly until dawn. Dolley, the most cheerful spouse in the history of the American presidency, did her best to keep his spirits high. At many of their weekly receptions, Madison managed to rise above his usual seriousness and engage in social conversation. But no one who knew him well could doubt that some part of his mind was constantly engaged with affairs of state. Released from all that strain, the Madisons spent the entire spring of 1815 at Montpelier.

Amid the turmoil of the previous years, Madison had come in for more than his fair share of criticism, not only from rabid Federalists but also from those who supported his basic policy while faulting his conduct of the war. But in the afterglow of peace and the patriotic sentiments it fostered, his countrymen found new affection for their President. He was, after all, one of a dwindling band of surviving Revolutionary leaders—and that alone commanded the respect of younger generations of Americans. All but his most embittered critics recognized that Madison's unstinting commitment to the principles of republican government and federal union somehow overshadowed lesser errors of judgment. As Abigail Adams had observed in February 1814, Madison reminded her of "what Pope called the noblest work of God: *an honest man.*"

During the final two years of his presidency, Madison at last had the chance to address domestic policy. His seventh and eighth annual messages to Congress proposed particular measures that he hoped would enable the United States to remain "in the tranquil enjoyment of prosperous and honorable peace." To arch-Republicans of the old school, Madison seemed to be flirting with Hamiltonian Federalism. This was especially the case with his proposal for rechartering a national bank; but it also seemed inherent in his support of both a limited tariff to protect new manufacturing industries and a constitutional amendment to enable the national government to undertake "internal improvements" through the building of roads and canals.

A quarter century earlier, Madison had opposed Hamilton's original plan for a bank on constitutional grounds. He had remained passive while Gallatin led the unsuccessful fight to recharter the national bank in 1811. But during the final year of the war, with the government relying on private banks to raise desperately needed loans, Madison had supported treasury secretary Dallas's effort to establish a second national bank before vetoing the measure that Congress eventually passed as inadequate. Now he made Dallas's proposal his own, happily signing the 1816 act establishing the Second Bank of the United States. The previous acceptance of the First Bank by all the branches of government, Madison reasoned, as well as evidence of popular support, had resolved the constitutional question in favor of the bank.

Madison thus allowed precedents set since 1789 to revise his own original understanding of the Constitution. But as his position on internal improvements made clear, he still opposed stretching the "necessary and proper" clause to justify any desired piece of legislation. As a matter of *policy*, Madison believed, roads and canals would prove as useful as a national bank, promoting economic growth and national integration. But rather than let policy alone set new precedents for loose construction, he preferred to remove doubts about the legitimacy of federal action through an appropriate constitutional amendment. Failing to grasp the importance Madison attached to this principle, Congress instead adopted an act applying profits from the Bank toward building roads and canals. On March 3, 1817, in his last official act, Madison vetoed this Bonus Bill as an improper attempt to exercise powers that the Constitution had not vested in Congress. The next day he watched as Monroe— who had narrowly won the Republican nomination over William Crawford, then easily defeated Rufus King, the Federalist candidate—took the oath of office.

Though less desperate to leave Washington than Jefferson had been eight years earlier, Madison clearly welcomed retirement. "I am in the midst of preparations to get to my farm, where I shall make myself a fixture," he wrote Gallatin (now minister to France) shortly after his term expired. The "many enjoyments" awaiting him at Montpelier, he noted, would "be a welcome exchange for the labors and anxieties of public life." After numerous farewell dinners, the Madisons finally left Washington (by steamboat) on April 6. One of those present on the first leg of their trip later recalled that Madison, just past his sixty-sixth birthday, "was as playful as a child; talked and joked with everybody on board, and reminded me of a schoolboy on a long vacation."

A long vacation it truly was: nearly twenty years would go by before Madison, the last survivor of all the great leaders of the Revolution, passed away. It was never a carefree vacation, however. For most of his retirement, Madison had to contend with the debts and declining economic circumstances that also harried Jefferson and Monroe in their final years. Like Jefferson, whom he visited regularly, Madison was a serious student of scientific agriculture. His letters after 1817 contain numerous discussions of crop rotation, fertilizer, plowing, and other details of Virginia farming; and in 1818, he even published a learned address on these topics that he had given as the newly elected president of the Agricultural Society of Albemarle. In his management of Montpelier, he actively applied progressive ideas about farming. Yet his best efforts could not spare him the declining grain and land prices and the bad harvests that sapped the economic vitality of Virginia. Nor did he have the heart to curb the most aggravating drain on his resources: the endless gambling debts run up by his absolute wastrel of a step-son, John Payne Todd. By the late 1820s Madison could maintain the comfortable life of the Virginia planter only by selling off land and other capital assets. For as long as he could, he avoided selling any of his aging work force of slaves. But by 1834, he felt he had no choice, and in a transaction that pained him deeply, he sold a number of slaves to a kinsman.

Even the most persistent dedication to his estate, however, left Madison free to devote long hours to reading and private correspondence. The latter had withered during his tenure as secretary of state; as President he had found it hard to take time even to write Jefferson. As an elder statesman, however, he now found himself asked to comment on events both current and historic. More than that, he recognized that much of his own and his generation's legacy would depend on the preserva-tion of accurate records of what they had accomplished. "The infant periods of most nations are buried in silence, or veiled in fable; and perhaps the world may have lost but little which it need regret," Madison observed in July 1819. But the founding of the American republic, he believed, would have unique importance for all mankind; "and, happily, there never was a case in which a knowledge of every interesting incident could be so accurately preserved." Having learned so much from the study of history, and recognizing that "personal knowledge [of events] and an impartial judgment of things rarely meet in the historian," he determined to "bequeath" to posterity materials that would enable later historians to write "unbiassed" accounts of the events in which he had played so prominent a part.

His most precious documents were his notes of the debates at the Federal Convention of 1787. Madison had long ruled out their publication while any of the framers were still alive. In part he felt bound to honor the delegates' original pledge of secrecy. But his deeper concern was political. From 1789 on, it had been evident that key clauses of the Constitution were subject to quite different interpretations. Madison feared that if the American public saw how these clauses had emerged from the intense bargaining of 1787, the authority of the Constitution itself might be reduced. The publication of the debates "should be delayed," he wrote in 1821, "till the Constitution should be well settled by practice, and till a knowledge of the controversial part of the proceedings of its framers can be turned to no improper account." Moreover, since Madison did not believe that the "intentions" of the framers should fix its "legitimate meaning," he saw no compelling reason to hasten publication.

Yet far from being "well settled by practice," the meaning of the Constitution seemed to grow more controversial, not less. "The Constitution itself," Madison observed in 1824, "must be an unfailing source of party distinctions." Within two years of his retirement, two great issues made Madison realize how divisive constitutional interpretation still remained.

The first of these issues involved the power of the Supreme Court and the jurisprudence of Chief Justice John Marshall. Like other Republicans, Madison was highly critical of the political role that Federalist judges had played during the late 1790s and even after the "Revolution of 1800." In 1803 he had himself been a party to the landmark decision in *Marbury* v. *Madison,* when the Court affirmed its authority to strike down acts of Congress as unconstitutional. But after 1814, the crucial use of the power of judicial review occurred when the Court voided acts of *state* legislation as contrary to the federal Constitution. In a series of major decisions involving appeals from the judgments of state courts—*Fairfax* v. *Hunter* (1818), *McCulloch* v. *Maryland* (1819), and *Cohens* v. *Virginia* (1821)—Marshall and Associate Justice Joseph Story established the supremacy of federal law over the legislative rights of the states. These decisions drew heated opposition from many Republicans, especially Spencer Roane of the Virginia Court of Appeals, who argued that the Supreme Court could not overturn decisions of state courts.

In support of their views, Roane and his allies looked back to the Virginia and Kentucky resolutions drafted by Madison and Jefferson two decades earlier, and they hoped to enlist the two former Presidents under the banner of state sovereignty. Madison sought to placate Roane by criticizing the Court's opinions on their merits. He particularly objected to the broad reading of the "necessary and proper" clause that the chief justice had offered in his *McCulloch* decision defending the constitutionality of the Bank of the United States. But when in 1821 Roane pressed him on the larger issue of the *right* of the Supreme Court to overrule state courts, Madison delivered a polite but firm rebuff. The "sounder policy" dictated that state claims had to yield to the principle of federal supremacy. And when Jefferson continued to voice support for Roane's position, Madison (not for the first time) took his old friend to task. Only federal judicial supremacy, Madison argued, could spare the Union the confusion and discord that would arise from any other method of resolving constitutional disputes. He thus held to the elegant but forceful conclusion he had reached in *Federalist* 39.

So, too, Madison returned to another opinion that had marked his constitutional thinking of the late 1780s. The states had more to fear from the *legislative* authority of Congress, Madison reminded Roane, than from the *judicial* decisions of the Marshall court, however erroneous. His concern on this point reflected the second great constitutional quarrel that erupted shortly after his retirement: the prolonged crisis of 1819–1821 over the admission of Missouri to the Union. As part of the enabling legislation, northern congressmen sought not only to prohibit the further migration of slaves into Missouri but also to provide for the emancipation of slave children in the territory. In the eventual Compromise, Missouri's admission as a slave state was balanced by the admission of Maine as a free state, while slavery was barred from the remaining portions of the Louisiana territory lying north of Missouri.

Madison condemned the entire northern effort as defective on constitutional grounds. Antislavery congressmen sought to govern the movement of slaves into the territories by invoking the murky clause allowing Congress (after 1808) to prohibit "the migration or importation of any such persons as any of the states now existing shall think proper to admit." Madison dismissed this claim as historically unsound. His notes from 1787 proved that the clause affected only the importation of slaves from overseas, not their domestic transportation. Applying his familiar rule of interpretation, he further argued that the southern states would never have adopted the Constitution had the clause been read in any other light. Nor could Congress restrict the right of a new state to adopt slavery, since that would "vary the political equality of the states."

But these constitutional claims only masked a more ominous political threat. "Parties under some denomination or other must always be expected in a government as free as ours," Madison observed in 1819. So he had argued in 1787, but now he carried his analysis a step further. When members of different parties were found throughout the country, they could actually work to "strengthen the union of the whole." But in the Missouri controversy, voting in Congress followed sectional lines. Here lay the great danger. "Should a state of parties arise, founded on geographical boundaries and other physical and permanent distinctions which happen to coincide with them, what is to control those great repulsive masses from awful shocks against each other?"

Among these "permanent distinctions," Madison now knew, the most important involved slavery. Once he had anticipated that the movement of population southwest would preserve a rough parity between the two sections of the Union in both houses of Congress. Such a balance would, he hoped, lead not to political stalemate but to mutual accommodation. But by the census of 1820, if not earlier, Madison knew that even the three-fifths rule could not prevent the South from becoming a permanent minority in the House. If slavery led to recurring conflict between the two great regions, what countervailing force would keep the Union together?

Madison's own thoughts about slavery followed the ideas that Jefferson had expressed in his *Notes on the State of Virginia*. While avoiding Jefferson's speculations about physical and mental differences between the races, he agreed that emancipation would require resettling the slaves elsewhere. Regarding the free blacks he observed as "idle and depraved," he feared that emancipated slaves would long remain "dissatisfied with their condition," a danger to "the ruling and privileged class" of whites. Thus, with other prominent leaders, Madison joined the colonization movement that led to the establishment of Liberia. But that, he knew, was a partial step affecting only a fraction of the blacks already freed. The emancipation of the remaining masses of plantation slaves would require years of sustained efforts to improve their moral condition as well as a *national* commitment to compensate the slaveholders for their property.

Such indefinite notions of emancipation went as far as all but the most radical opponents of slavery were prepared to go in the 1820s. Madison saw slavery as a moral and humanitarian issue—"the dreadful calamity which has so long afflicted our country and filled so many with despair." By all accounts, his treatment of his own slaves at Montpelier was exemplary in every respect short of emancipation. But after 1819, he understood that slavery had emerged, first and foremost, as a *political* issue threatening the Union. Viewed in this way, the future solution of the slavery problem required its northern critics to accept the reality of its current importance to the South. That acceptance had been part of the original constitutional compact of 1787–1788; for the North to violate it now, Madison felt, would amount to renouncing the Union itself. And this in turn explains why the decisions of the Marshall Court so alarmed him. For southern allegiance to the Union could no longer be assured if a northern-dominated Congress actively wielded the broad legislative powers the Court seemed disposed to recognize.

Yet this same commitment to the Union also led Madison to repudiate the growth of states'-rights sentiment in the South, as expressed first by Spencer Roane and his circle, and then by the South Carolina radicals grouped around John C. Calhoun, who opposed the protectionist tariff of 1828 with the claim that a state could nullify an act of Congress it deemed unconstitutional. Pained by their repeated appeals to the Virginia and Kentucky resolutions, Madison struggled to make his correspondents aware that the American federal system he had done so much to create could not survive repeated efforts to reduce its complexities to the simplistic formulas of state sovereignty or unrestricted national supremacy.

In the final years of his life, James Madison thus found himself returning to precisely the same difficult issues that had preoccupied him in 1787. Now, as then, he sought to map a "middle ground" between an effective national government and the residual powers of the states. Time and again, in letters to partisans on both sides of the question, he explained why American federalism could never be described in neat or tidy terms. It was neither the "consolidated government" that southerners feared nor the traditional confederation of sovereign states that they sought to defend. The American federal system "is so unexampled in its origin, so complex in its structure, and so peculiar in some of its features," he reminded Daniel Webster in 1830, "that in describing it the political vocabulary does not furnish terms sufficiently distinctive and appropriate, without a detailed resort to the facts of the case." On one point, however, Madison was insistent. The inevitable conflicts that would arise from the overlapping powers of the nation and the states must be left to the Supreme Court. That had been the original understanding of 1787–1788, and events since then had, if anything, convinced him that no other solution could better maintain the integrity of the federal Union. But in truth, he also believed, the preservation of the Union required patience and accommodation on all sides.

All his life, Madison had approached political problems with a quizzical intelligence that preferred careful distinctions to simple formulations. That was what set him apart from Jefferson, whose mind ranged more widely, he knew, but who was also prone to sudden enthusiasms and a tendency to express "in strong and round terms, impressions of the moment." The error of this approach was that it asked more of Americans than their political system could support. For in the end the central challenge to the Constitution and the Union was a stark one: could either survive in a society that was half-slave, half-free?

His mind was vigorous to the end, and as long as his body could keep up, Madison remained active. No one should think that his retirement had given him "leisure for whatever pursuit might be most inviting," he observed in 1827. "The truth, however, is that I have rarely . . . found my time less at my disposal than since I took my leave" from public office. Passing dignitaries, friends, and his numerous relations all visited Montpelier, while "the cares incident to the perplexing species of labor and of husbandry" on which his fortunes rested took constant attention. Rheumatism made the task of keeping up with his correspondence more time-consuming.

Nor was he wholly free of public obligations. Since 1816 he had been a member of the board of visitors for Jefferson's last great project, the University of Virginia at Charlottesville, just below the great house at Monticello. The task was by no means an easy one. In the hard times of the 1820s, the Virginia legislature was slow to appropriate needed funds, while Jefferson and Madison faced opposition from sectarian groups critical of their refusal to give the teaching of religion any place in the university curriculum. But however great the obstacles, meetings of the board of visitors were always welcome because they allowed the Madisons to visit the sage of Monticello. On one memorable occasion in November 1824, Madison joined Jefferson at a public dinner honoring the Marquis de Lafayette during his tour of America. The hundreds of well-wishers attending the dinner sensed the passing of the remarkable generation they had been raised to revere. But their feelings of curiosity and respect paled next to the powerful emotions of the aging revolutionaries themselves.

The three men and Monroe met again in August 1825, shortly before Lafayette returned to France. By then Madison sensed that Jefferson, bankrupt and feeble, was fading. In February 1826, a letter from Monticello signaled farewell. "The friendship which has persisted between us, now half a century, and the harmony of our political principles and pursuits, have been sources of constant happiness to me through that long period," Jefferson wrote. "To myself you have been a pillar of support through life. Take care of me when dead, and be assured that I shall leave with you my last affections." Madison replied in kind. "You cannot look back to the long period of our private friendship and political harmony, with more affecting recollections than I do," he wrote. "If they are a source of pleasure to you, what ought they not to be to me?"

Their friendship—surely the most remarkable (if not indeed admirable) in American political history—came to its end on the fiftieth anniversary of the Declaration of Independence, when to the wonderment of all, Jefferson and John Adams passed away within hours of each other. Madison honored the request to look after Jefferson's reputation, and also took over his place as rector of the university. One other public duty came his way in the fall of 1829, when, accompanied by Dolley, he attended the convention drafting a new state constitution at Richmond as a delegate from Orange County. There, with his colleagues gathered around his chair to catch his faint voice, he gave his last political speech supporting a proposal that would reduce the disproportionate influence that tidewater planters held in the lower house of assembly by virtue of being able to count all their slaves for purposes of representation.

Physical debility and bouts of illness sharply curbed his activities thereafter. Yet even after he passed his eightieth birthday in March 1831, Madison's interest in national politics remained undiminished. As the nullification crisis mounted in 1832 and 1833, he repeatedly wrote his Washington correspondents to condemn the "monstrous" heresies emanating from South Carolina, and to explain in chapter and verse why the Virginia and Kentucky resolutions of 1798 could never condone the idea that a single state could nullify national law.

He had been the sole surviving framer of the Constitution since 1828. With the passing of James Monroe in 1831 and Charles Carroll, the last signer of the Declaration, the next year, he remained the only prominent Revolutionary leader still alive. "Having outlived so many of my cotemporaries," he observed in 1831, "I ought not to forget that I may be thought to have outlived myself." In 1834 Madison drafted a short memorandum of "Advice to my Country," which concluded with an admonition "that the union of the states be cherished and perpetuated." But his final testament remained his notes of the debates at the Constitutional Convention, whose publication he authorized Dolley to oversee when he dictated his last will on the sixtieth anniversary of the outbreak of the Revolutionary War. Among all the purposes he hoped these notes would serve, the most important was to leave his countrymen the exemplary evidence of how his generation, through political reason and compromise, had overcome divisions as severe as any he had observed in his retirement.

It was the tragedy of his declining years that events left him to doubt whether the generations to come after would master the lesson.

Death came on June 28, 1836. As the story was told, his favorite niece, Nelly Willis, was watching Madison eat his breakfast when she noticed a slight change of expression cross his face. Was anything wrong? she asked. "Nothing more than a change of mind, my dear," he replied. And then "his head instantly dropped, and he ceased breathing as quickly as the snuff of a candle goes out." Thus, thoughtful to the last, ended the life of James Madison—not, perhaps, the new republic's greatest leader, but certainly its most powerful and probing political intellect.

A Note on the Sources

The active political career of James Madison lasted more than four decades, during which he participated in nearly every event of any significance. No short bibliographic note can do justice to the extensive primary sources—both archival and published—and massive body of historical writings that bear on his career. Accordingly, this note describes only those sources and works that relate most directly to this book.

Madison took care to preserve his most valuable political papers, but after his death the financial needs of his widow and especially of his stepson, John Payne Todd, led to the sale of numerous manuscripts to individual collectors. By far the largest collection of Madison papers is found in the Library of Congress. Spanning his entire career, it is readily accessible to scholars on microfilm. Numerous libraries and historical societies have small Madison holdings. Perhaps the most notable of these is a group of letters to William Pinkney, the American minister in London during Madison's tenure as secretary of state, in the William Pinkney Papers at Princeton University.

Fortunately, most of Madison's writings have already been printed or will be published in the current edition of his papers: William T. Hutchinson, William M. E. Rachal, Robert A. Rutland *et al.*, eds., *The Papers of James Madison* (Chicago and Charlottesville, 1962–   ). To date, fifteen volumes of Madison's papers down to 1795 have appeared, as well as the introductory volumes of two separate series covering his terms as secretary of state and President. This edition already supersedes the first five volumes of Gaillard Hunt, ed. *The Writings of James Madison*, 9 v. (New York, 1900–1910), whose later volumes are also inferior to William C. Rives and Philip R. Fendall, eds., *Letters and Other Writings of James Madison*, 4 v. (Philadelphia, 1865), particularly for the extensive and revealing correspondence of Madison's retirement.

The one phase of Madison's career that has been studied most closely is the period of the adoption of the Constitution. His notes of debates and his own speeches at the Constitutional Convention are found in Max Farrand, ed., *The Records of the Federal Convention of 1787,* 4 v., rev. ed. (New Haven, 1937). His contributions to *The Federalist* can be found in v. 10 of *The Papers of James Madison,* but are probably better read in any of the modern editions of that work, notably those prepared by Jacob Cooke (Middletown, Conn., 1961); Benjamin F. Wright (Cambridge, 1961); or Isaac Kramnick (New York, 1988). Madison's crucial role in the ratification of the Constitution in Virginia can be traced in John P. Kaminski and Gaspare J. Saladino, eds., *The Documentary History of the Ratification of the Constitution,* v. 8–10 (Madison, 1989–1990).

Only Madison's major speeches in the Federal Congress after 1789 are reprinted in the respective editions of his *Papers* and *Writings,* making it necessary to consult the fuller (though often less than accurate) records in the *Annals of Congress.* For his diplomatic correspondence after 1801, the *American State Papers, Foreign Relations,* is equally necessary but similarly flawed; scholars prefer to use the original manuscript records of the Department of State in the National Archives.

A useful short collection of some of Madison's most important papers is Marvin Meyers, ed., *The Mind of the Founder: Sources of the Political Thought of James Madison,* rev. ed. (Hanover, N.H., 1981). No correspondence in American history can rival that between Madison and Jefferson, which is why the anticipated publication of James Morton Smith's comprehensive edition of their letters will be a notable literary event.

All students of Madison's career owe a major debt to Irving Brant's *James Madison,* 6 v. (Indianapolis, 1941–1961); a one-volume condensation appeared in 1970. Brant's extensive chronicle offers shrewd insights into Madison's behavior, always favorable to his subject; but scholars have questioned his views on many points of interpretation, especially his treatment of Madison's nationalism. The best single-volume biography is Ralph Ketcham, *James Madison: A Biography* (New York, 1971), which manages to be consistently sympathetic yet balanced. Harold Schultz, *James Madison* (New York, 1970) provides a compact treatment of his political career. Robert A. Rutland, *James Madison: The Founding Father* (New York, 1987), is a lively account that begins (rather curiously) with the struggle to ratify the Constitution. Drew R. McCoy, *The Last of the Fathers: James Madison and the Republican Legacy* (New York, 1989), appeared too late to be used for this study, but provides a powerful analysis of the aging statesman's poignant reflections on the fate of the republic. Also valuable are two interpretive studies by Adrienne Koch, *Madison's Advice to My Country* (Princeton, 1966), and *Jefferson and Madison: The Great Collaboration* (New York, 1950); and Edward M. Burns, *James Madison: Philosopher of the Constitution* (New Brunswick, 1938), which was perhaps the first work to call attention to the importance of Madison's political thought.

More influential in this respect, however, were several essays by the historian Douglass Adair, which are gathered in Trevor Colbourn, ed., *Fame and the Founding Fathers: Essays by Douglass Adair* (New York, 1974). Nearly as important were essays by the political theorist Martin Diamond, most notably "Democracy and *The Federalist:* A Reconsideration of the Framers' Intent," *American Political Science Review,* 53 (1959), 52–68. Together, Adair and Diamond màde the theoretical sophistication and originality of Madison's contributions to *The Federalist* evident to a wider community of scholars, who have since turned the analysis of that work into something of a cottage industry. The most important commentaries on *The Federalist* include David F. Epstein, *The Political Theory of The Federalist* (Chicago, 1984); the essays collected in Charles R. Kesler, ed., *Saving the Revolution: The Federalist Papers [sic] and the American Founding* (New York, 1987); Morton White, *Philosophy, The Federalist and the Constitution* (New York, 1987); and the quirky work of Garry Wills, *Explaining America: The Federalist* (Garden City, N.Y., 1981). Three important interpretive essays are Robert J. Morgan, "Madison's Theory of Representation in the Tenth Federalist," *Journal of Politics,* 36 (1974), 852–885; Jean

Yarbrough, "Representation and Republicanism: Two Views," *Publius*, 9 (1979), 77–98; and Daniel W. Howe, "The Political Psychology of *The Federalist*," *William and Mary Quarterly*, 3rd ser., 44 (1987), 485–509.

It would be a serious error, however, to equate the sum of Madison's political theory with his writings as Publius; his contributions to *The Federalist* mark only one phase in the larger evolution of his ideas and concerns. Most historians accordingly prefer to locate the development of Madison's thought in the context of his political involvements, especially during the two crucial decades of the 1780s and 1790s. I have drawn extensively on my own treatment of Madison in *The Beginnings of National Politics: An Interpretive History of the Continental Congress* (New York, 1979), and several essays written concurrently with this book: "Mr. Meese, Meet Mr. Madison," *Atlantic* (December 1986) 77–86; "The Great Compromise: Ideas, Interests, and the Politics of Constitution Making," *William and Mary Quarterly*, 3d ser., 44 (1987), 424–457; "The Structure of Politics at the Accession of George Washington," in Richard Beeman *et al.*, eds., *Beyond Confederation: Origins of the Constitution and American National Identity* (Chapel Hill, 1987); "The Madisonian Moment," *University of Chicago Law Review*, 55 (1988), 473–505; and, with Susan Zlomke, "James Madison and the Independent Executive," *Presidential Studies Quarterly*, 16 (1987), 293–300.

At the same time, I have learned much from (but not always agreed with) the writings of many colleagues. Three essays by Lance Banning offer some differences of emphasis from my own interpretations: "James Madison and the Nationalists, 1780–1783," *William and Mary Quarterly*, 3d ser., 40 (1983), 227–255; "The Hamiltonian Madison," *Virginia Magazine of History and Biography* 92 (1984), 3–28; and "The Practicable Sphere of a Republic: James Madison, the Constitutional Convention, and the Emergence of Revolutionary Federalism," in Beeman, ed., *Beyond Confederation*. This last volume also contains a valuable essay by Drew R. McCoy, "James Madison and Visions of American Nationality in the Confederation Period: A Regional Perspective." The crucial place of the proposed veto on state laws is ably explicated in Charles F. Hobson, "The Negative on

State Laws: James Madison, the Constitution, and the Crisis of Republican Government," *William and Mary Quarterly,* 3d ser., 36 (1979), 215–235. A stimulating essay by John Zvesper, "The Madisonian Systems," *Western Political Quarterly,* 37 (1984), 236–255, analyzes the apparent "inconsistency" between his efforts to control faction in 1787 and his role in the founding of the opposition Republican party during the 1790s. Deeper consistencies in Madison's vision of republican politics and the national interest are explored in two monographs on the political economy of the early republic. Drew R. McCoy, *The Elusive Republic: Political Economy in Jeffersonian America* (Chapel Hill, 1979) argues that Madison and Jefferson sought to pursue a middle path that would promote American economic development without incurring the social costs and political corruption they associated with Europe and Britain. John R. Nelson, Jr., *Liberty and Property: Political Economy and Policymaking in the New Nation, 1789–1812* (Baltimore, 1987) effectively challenges the idea that the Republican leaders opposed the development of American manufacturing. Republican economic ideas are also examined in Joyce Appleby, *Capitalism and a New Social Order: The Republican Vision of the 1790s* (New York, 1984).

A comprehensive bibliography of works relating to Madison's political career would necessarily include a staggering number of historical narratives, monographs, and biographies. Only the works that have been relevant to this book will be listed here.

Virginia politics are well treated in Charles Sydnor's *Gentlemen Freeholders: Political Practices in Washington's Virginia* (Chapel Hill, 1952); Norman K. Risjord, *Chesapeake Politics, 1781–1800* (New York, 1978); and Richard R. Beeman, *The Old Dominion and the New Nation, 1788–1801* (Lexington, Ky., 1972). For the politics of the Confederation era, see (in addition to Rakove, *Beginnings of National Politics*): Peter S. Onuf, *The Origins of the Federal Republic: Jurisdictional Controversies in the United States, 1775–1787* (Philadelphia, 1983); Merrill Jensen, *The New Nation: A History of the United States during the Confederation, 1781–1789* (New York, 1950); Forrest McDonald, *E Pluribus Unum: The Formation of the American Republic, 1776–1790,* rev. ed., (Indianapolis, 1979); H. James Henderson, *Party Politics in the Continental Congress* (New York, 1974); E. James Ferguson, *The Power of the Purse: A History of American Public Finance, 1776–1790* (Chapel Hill, 1961); and Frederick W. Marks, III, *Independence on Trial: Foreign Affairs and the Making of the Constitution* (Baton Rouge, 1973).

Although there are numerous narrative accounts of the Federal Convention, none can take the place of Madison's original notes of debates, which is the source on which all writers, both scholarly and popular, depend. As an alternative to the Farrand edition of the Convention records (cited above), see the one-volume edition of Adrienne Koch, ed., *Notes of Debates in the Federal Convention of 1787; Reported by James Madison* (Athens, Ohio, 1966). For the intellectual background to the Convention, Gordon S. Wood, *The Creation of the American Republic, 1776–1787* (Chapel Hill, 1969) is indispensable, particularly because Wood's dominant concern with the character of the state constitutions tracks Madison's own analysis at crucial points. Also valuable is Willi Paul Adams, *The First American Constitutions: Republican Ideology and the Making of the State Constitutions in the Revolutionary Era,* trans. Robert and Rita Kimber (Chapel Hill, 1980). The ratification struggle is surveyed in Robert A. Rutland, *The Ordeal of the Constitution* (Norman, Okla., 1966).

The development of the first political party system has been the subject of extensive analysis, much of it ably synthesized in Richard Hofstadter, *The Idea of a Party System* (Berkeley and Los Angeles, 1969). Madison's leading role in the formation of the opposition to the Federalists is traced in Noble E. Cunningham, Jr., *The Jeffersonian Republicans: The Formation of Party Organization, 1789–1801* (Chapel Hill, 1957), though he figures less prominently in the sequel, *The Jefferson Republicans in Power: Party Operations, 1801–1809* (Chapel Hill, 1963). As their subtitles suggest, Lance Banning, *The Jeffersonian Persuasion: Evolution of Party Ideology* (Ithaca, N.Y., 1978), and Richard Buel, Jr., *Securing the Revolution: Ideology in American Politics, 1789–1815* (Ithaca, N.Y., 1972) are concerned more with the values and beliefs undergirding the parties than with the ongoing conduct of politics. A matched pair of books by Forrest McDonald, *The Presidency of George Washington* (Lawrence, Kansas, 1974) and *The Presidency of Thomas Jefferson* (Lawrence, Kansas, 1976) cast a cold eye on the Republicans both in and out of power. James Morton Smith, *Freedom's Fetters: The Alien and Sedition Laws and American Civil Liberties* (Ithaca, N.Y., 1956) is the standard history of the crisis of the late 1790s.

The relation between foreign affairs and domestic politics during the first quarter century of government under the Constitution has been closely examined in a number of works. Jerald A. Combs, *The Jay Treaty: Political Battleground of the Founding Fathers* (Berkeley and Los Angeles, 1970) traces the explosive impact of that negotiation on American politics. Relations with France are the subject of three volumes by Alexander DeConde: *Entangling Alliance: Politics & Diplomacy under George Washington* (Durham, N.C., 1958); *The Quasi-War: The Politics and Diplomacy of the Undeclared War with France, 1797–1801* (New York, 1966); and *This Affair of Louisiana* (New York, 1976). Those with Britain are similarly examined in three works by Bradford Perkins that are frequently critical of Jefferson and Madison's diplomacy: *The First Rapprochement: England and the United States, 1795–1805* (Philadelphia, 1953); *Prologue to War: England and the United States, 1805–1812* (Berkeley and Los Angeles, 1961); *Castelreagh and Adams: England and the United States, 1812–1823* (Berkeley and Los Angeles, 1964).

Burton Spivack, *Jefferson's English Crisis: Commerce, Embargo, and the Republican Revolution* (Charlottesville, 1979), takes a critical look at the events that launched the Republican administrations on their troubled course toward war. Even more important, however, is J. C. A. Stagg, *Mr. Madison's War: Politics, Diplomacy, and Warfare in the Early Republic, 1783–1830* (Princeton, 1983), a prodigiously researched book that casts the decision for war in 1812 in the broad context of Madison's political economy, the development of Canada, and the complexities of party politics and the constitutional system, while leaving ample room for the military history of the war itself. Also valuable are Roger H. Brown, *The Republic in Peril: 1812* (New York, 1964), and Ronald L. Hatzenbuehler and Robert L. Ivie, *Congress Declares War: Rhetoric, Leadership, and Partisanship in the Early Republic* (Kent, Ohio, 1983).

Regrettably, there is no study of the Madison presidency equivalent to Noble E. Cunningham, Jr., *The Process of Government under Jefferson* (Princeton, 1978), Robert M. Johnstone, Jr., *Jefferson and the Presidency: Leadership in the Young Republic* (Ithaca, N.Y., 1978). Ralph Ketcham, *Presidents Above Party: The First American Presidency, 1789–1829* (Chapel Hill, 1984), is suggestive but lacks detail on Madison—somewhat surprisingly, given Ketcham's earlier biography.

Finally, no bibliography would be complete without reference to Henry Adams's incomparable *History of the United States during the Administrations of Jefferson and Madison,* 10 v. (New York, 1889–1891), still a classic of American historiography.

Acknowledgments

The writing of this book coincided with my intense (some say too intense) participation in the full panoply of activities associated with the bicentennial of the Constitution. These engagements delayed the completion of this book, but they also afforded me valuable opportunities to express, develop, and refine my ideas about James Madison. I am accordingly grateful to the organizers and hosts of the various conferences and lectures where I was able to present my thoughts. Oscar Handlin was an exemplary editor; from his demanding eye, I now know, even Madison would have benefited. Michael Holt and John Stagg saved me (I hope) from serious misjudgments. The manuscript was completed during a term at the Stanford Humanities Center, where Dee Marquez proved especially helpful.

My family distracted me from my work in ingenious ways. Helen kept me laughing, which probably contributed to a net productivity gain. Daniel often convinced me I would do better work after pitching batting practice to him. Robby at least lent me his considerable expertise on the naval aspects of the War of 1812. At a much earlier stage, he asked me, "Daddy, do you still have ideas, or do you make it up?" After that, I realized I was ready for anything the most benighted reviewer might say.

Jack N. Rakove

Index